AF496512

– As for the future.

Annette Heyer

The Fruitmarket Gallery, Edinburgh

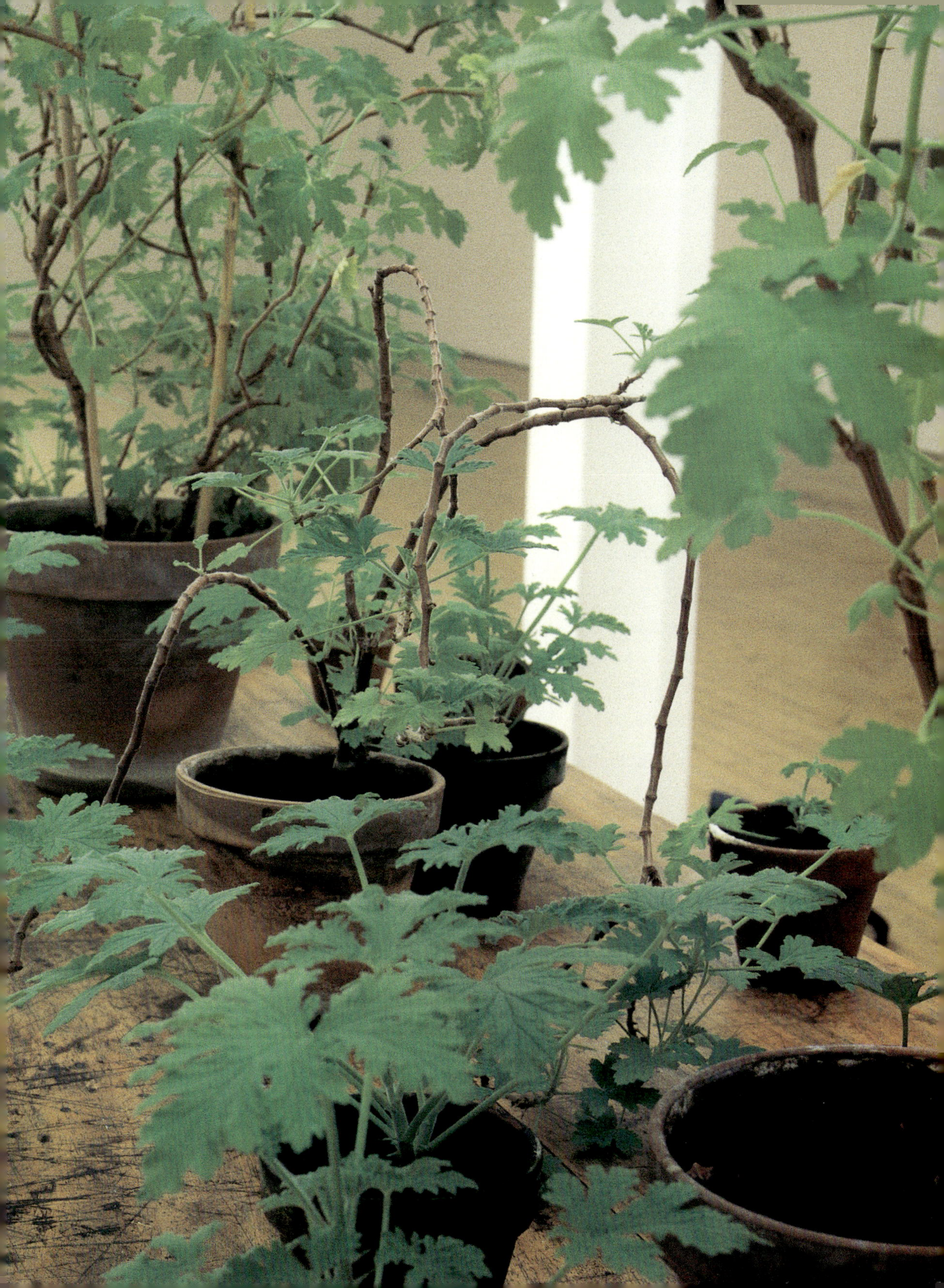

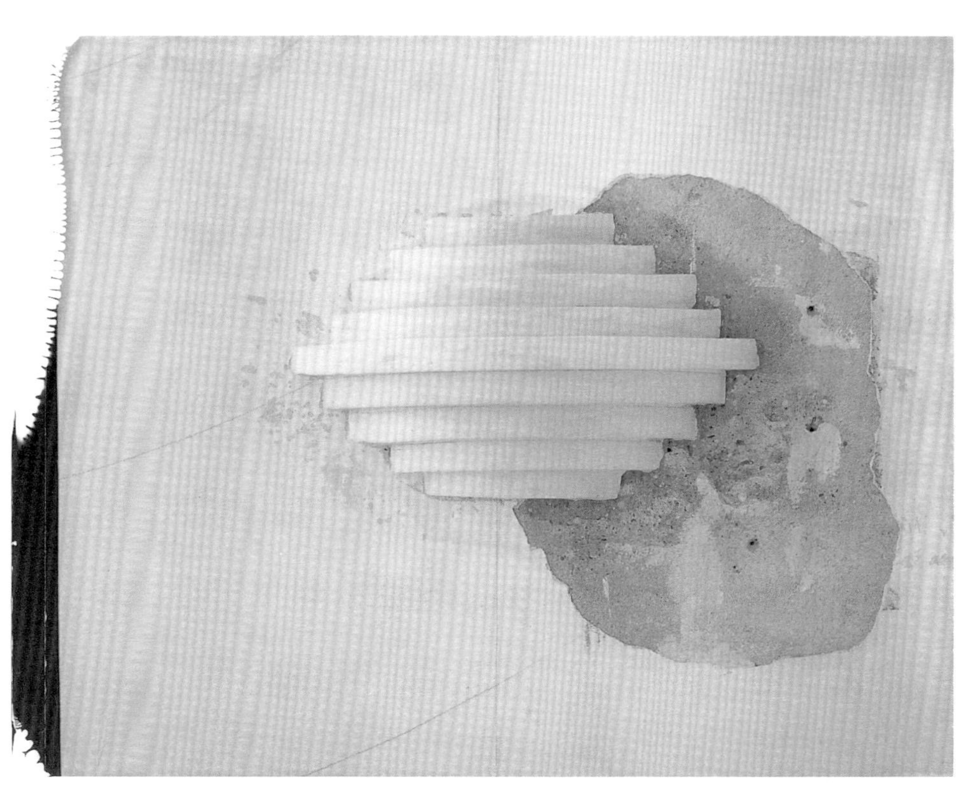

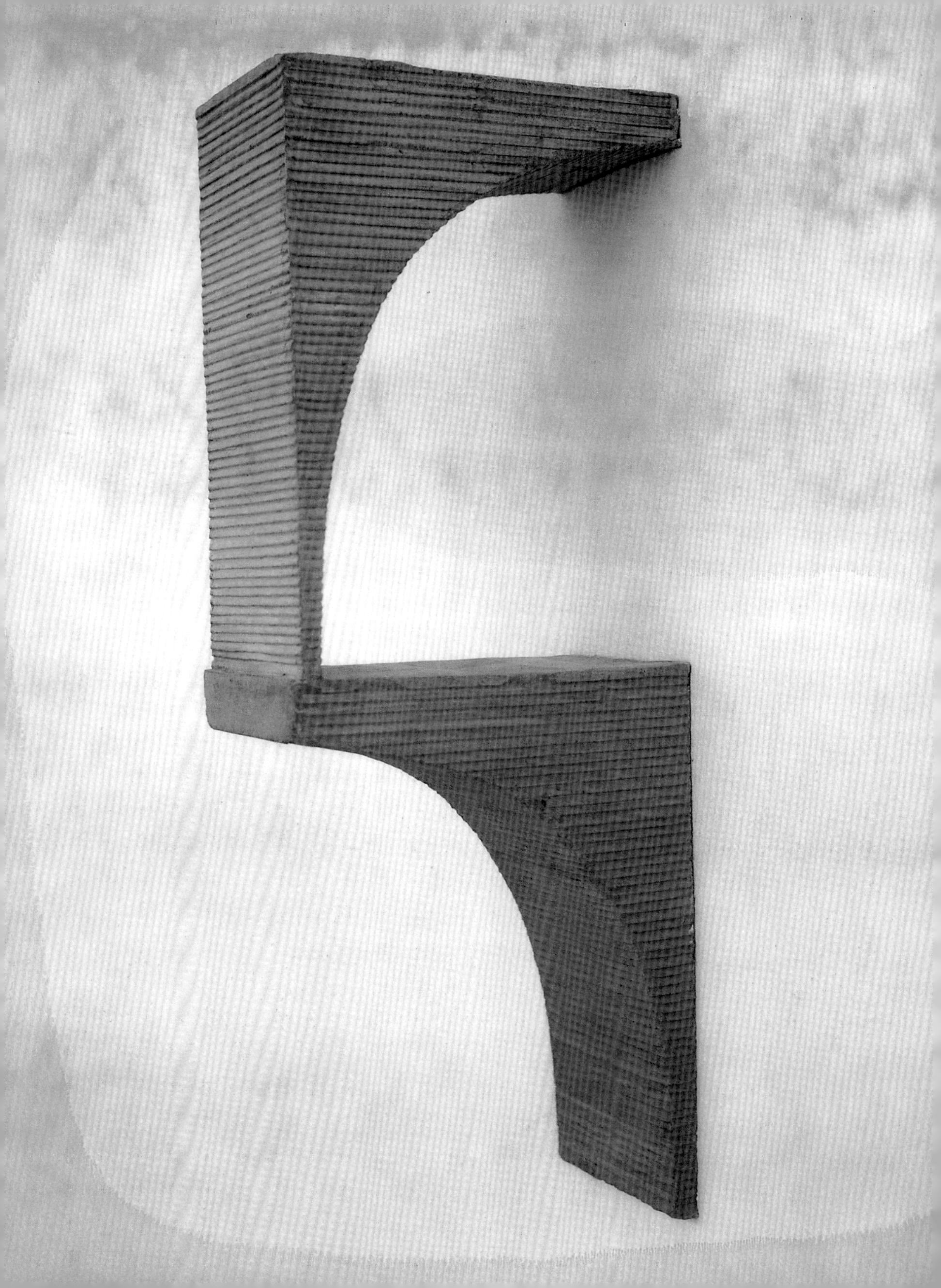

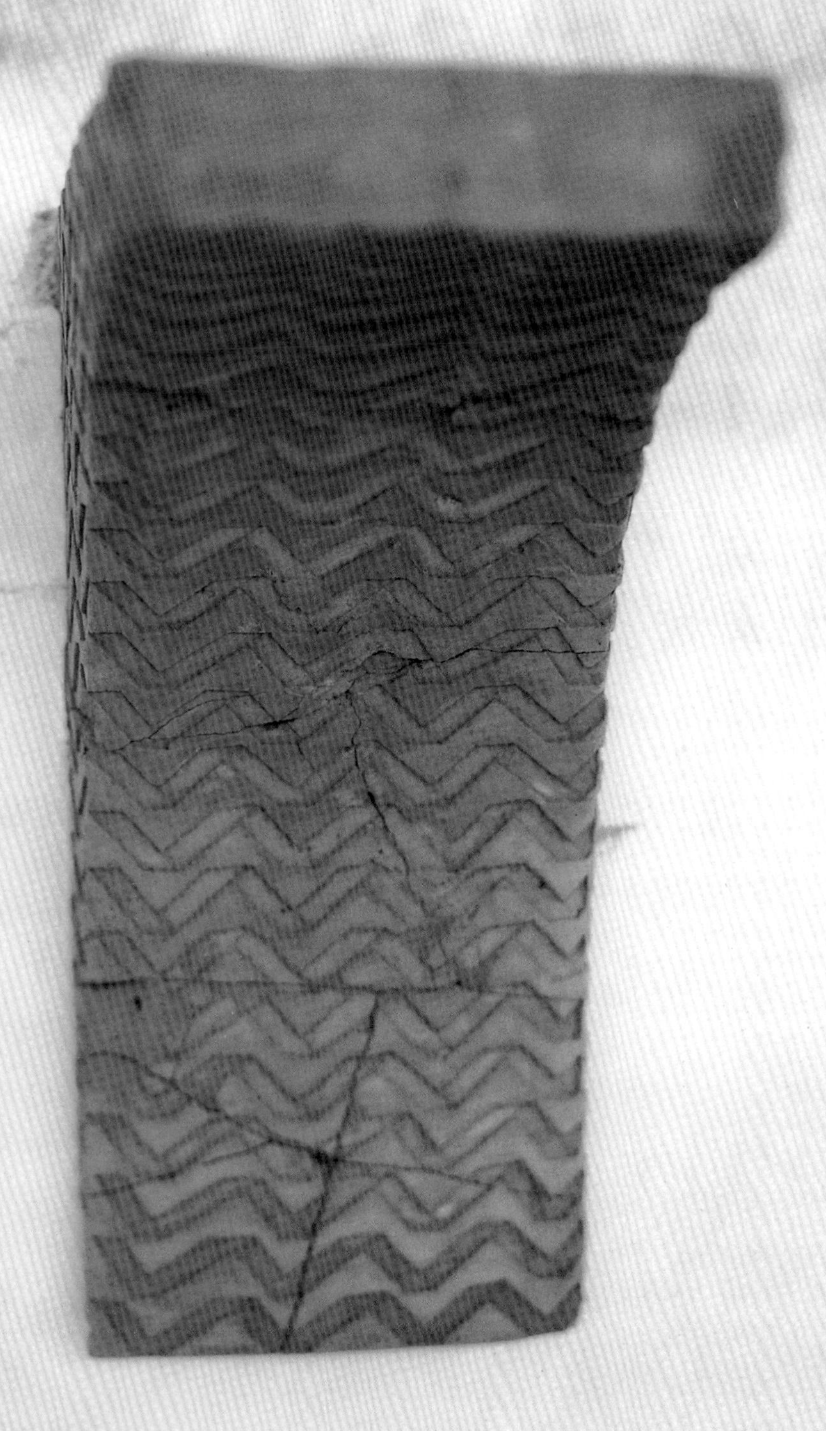

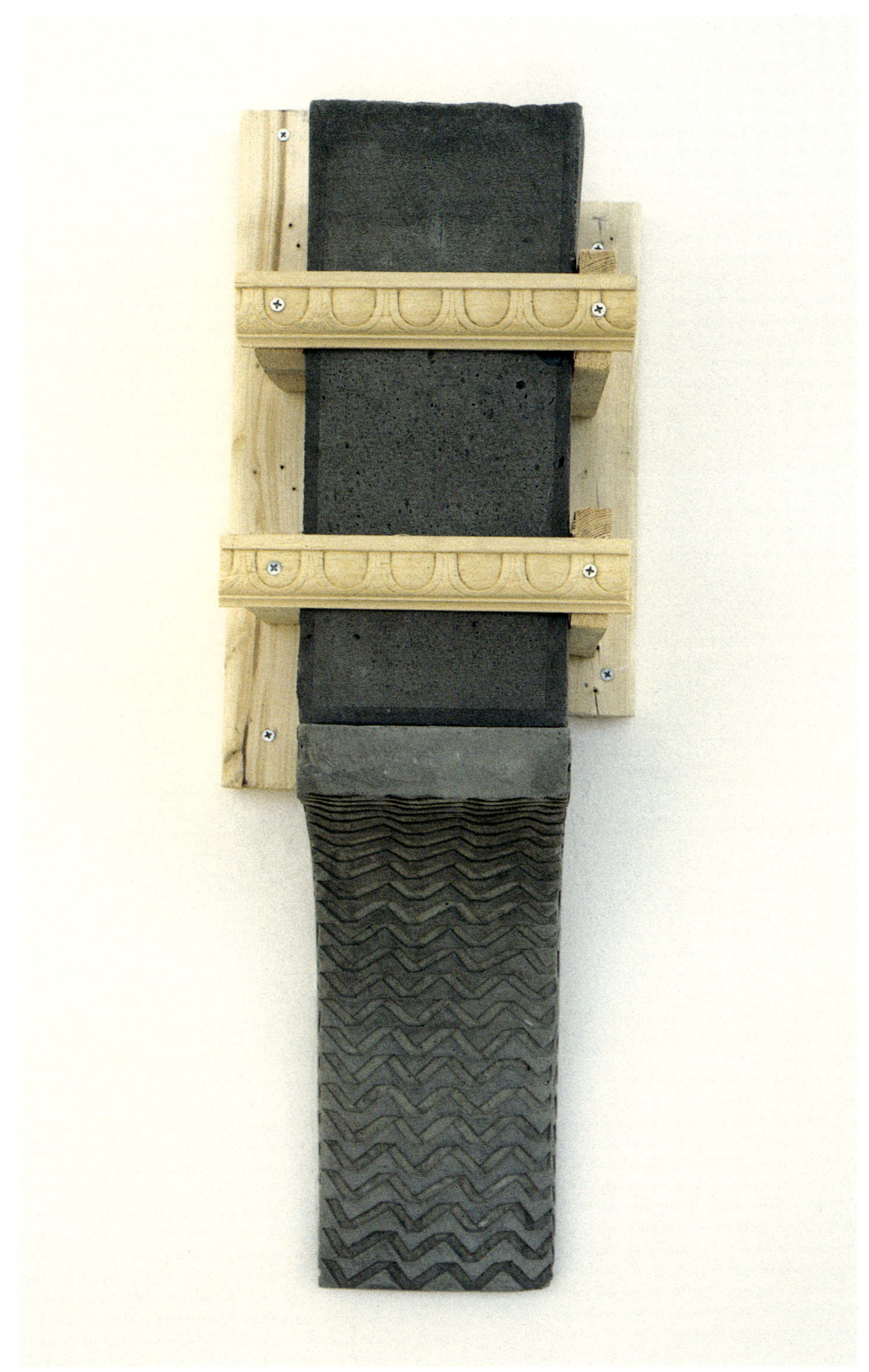

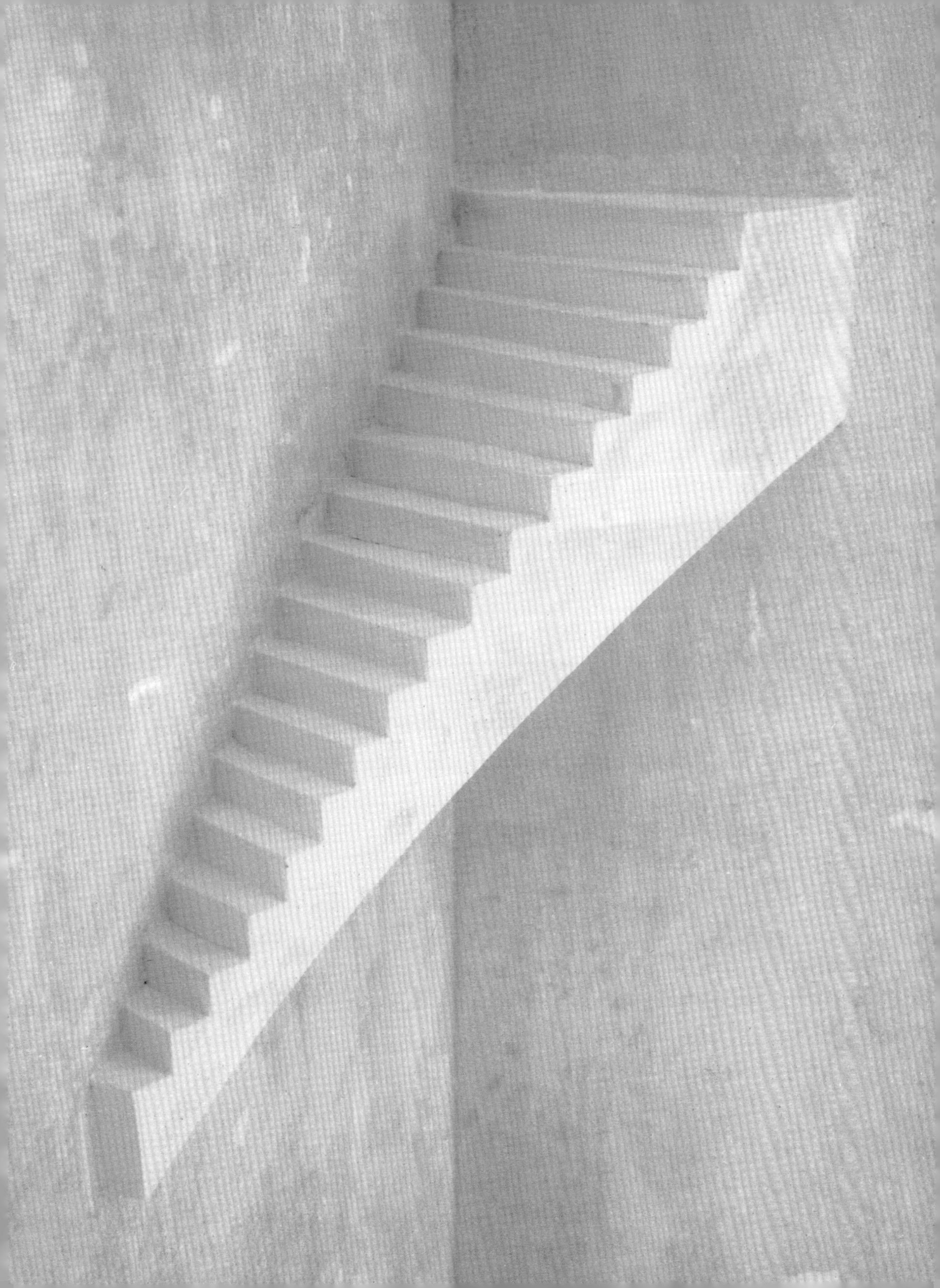

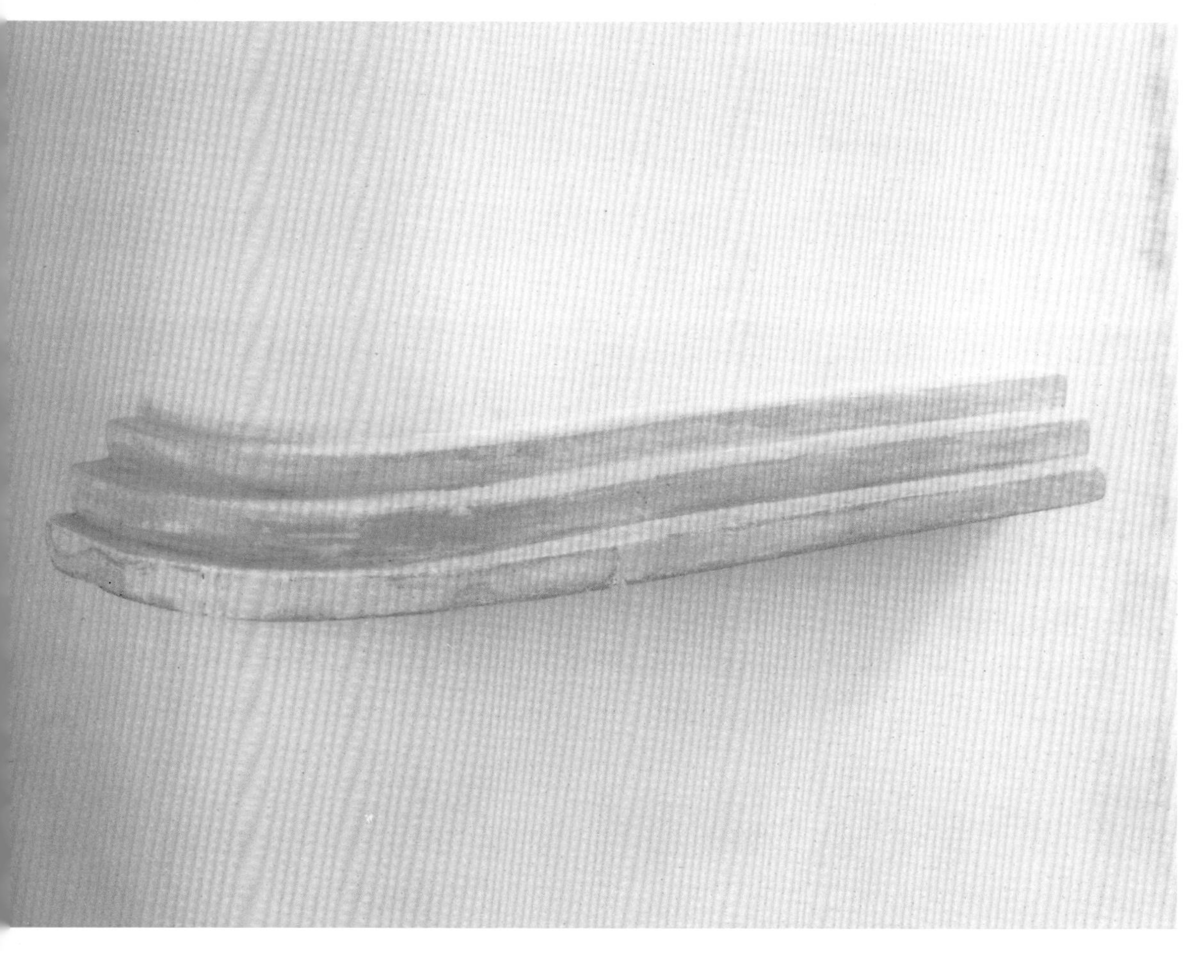

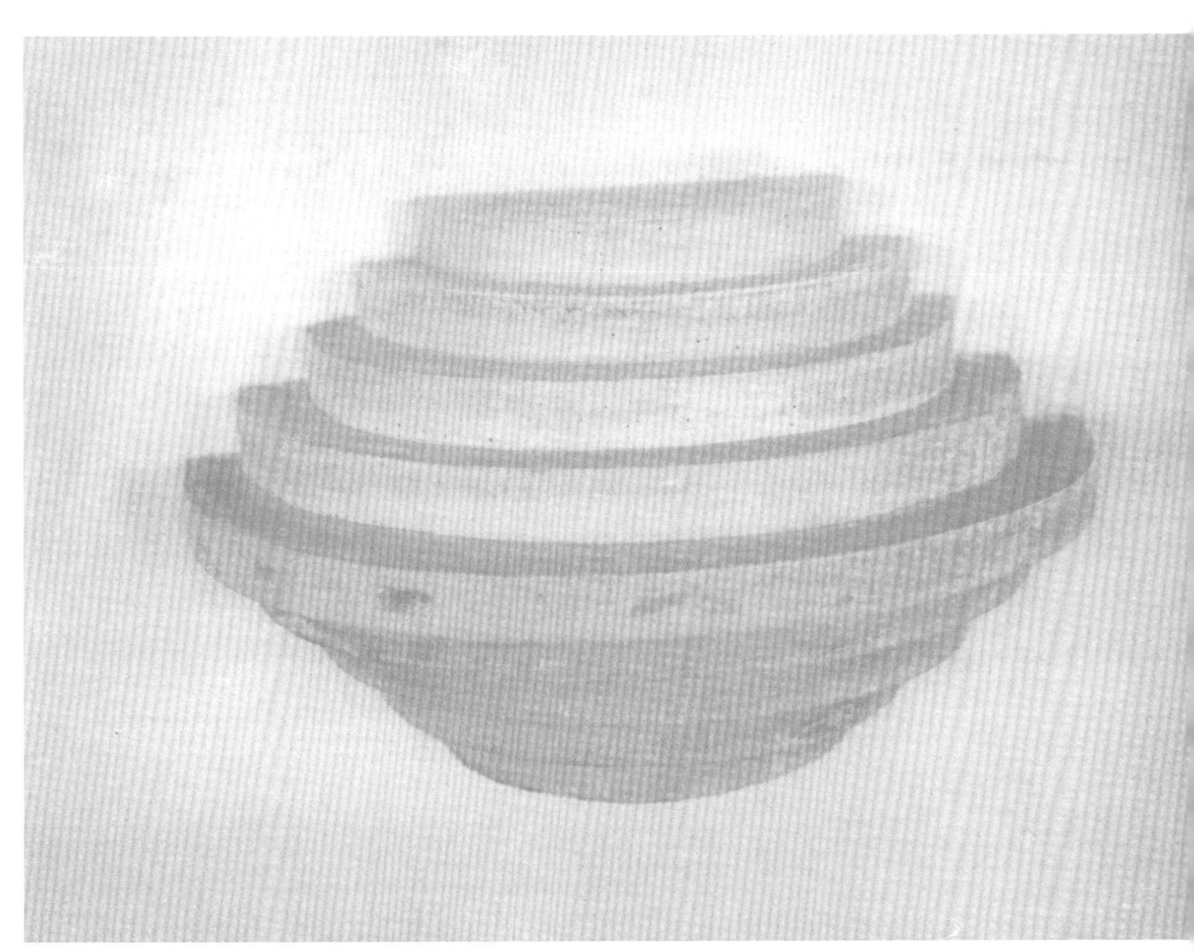

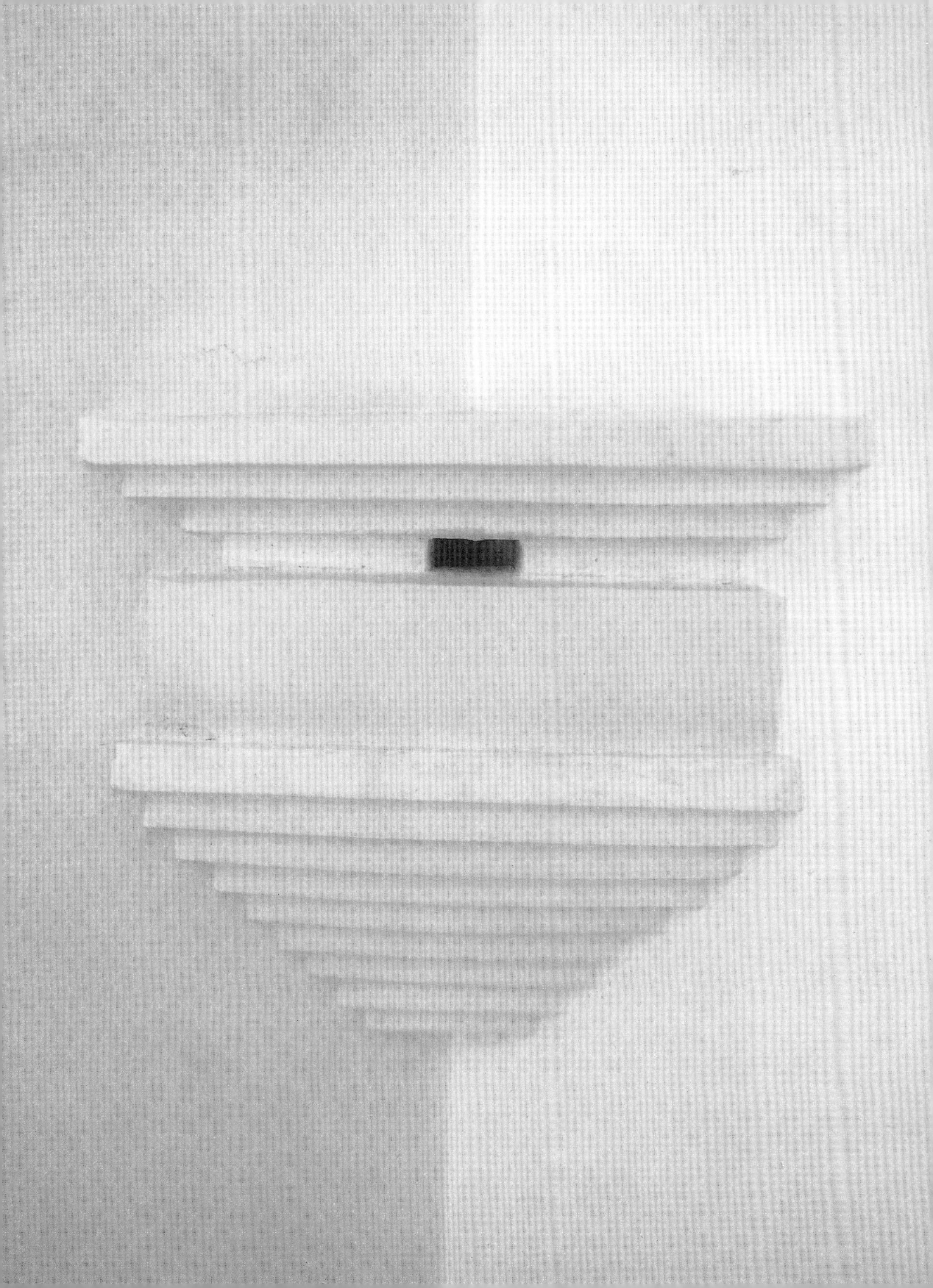

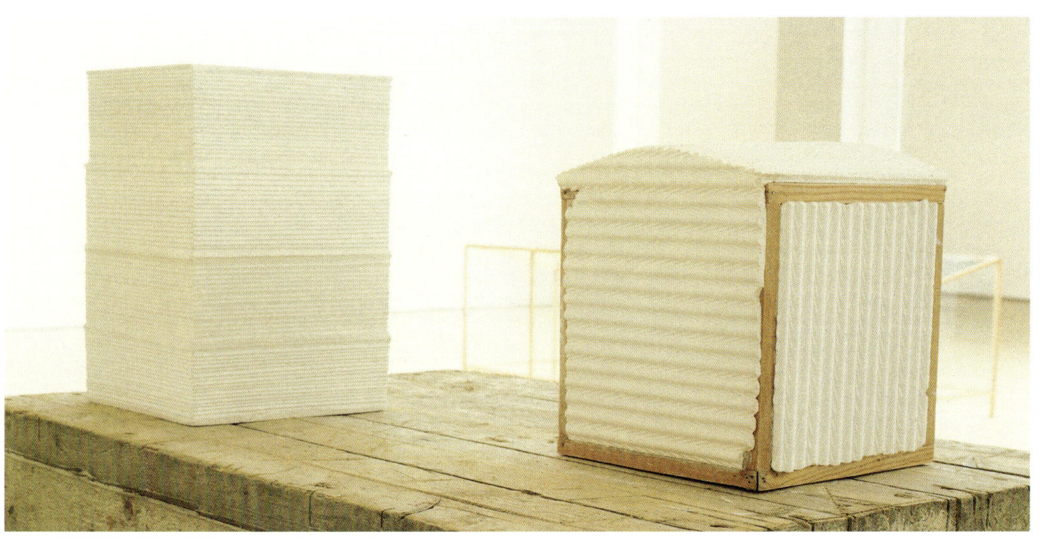

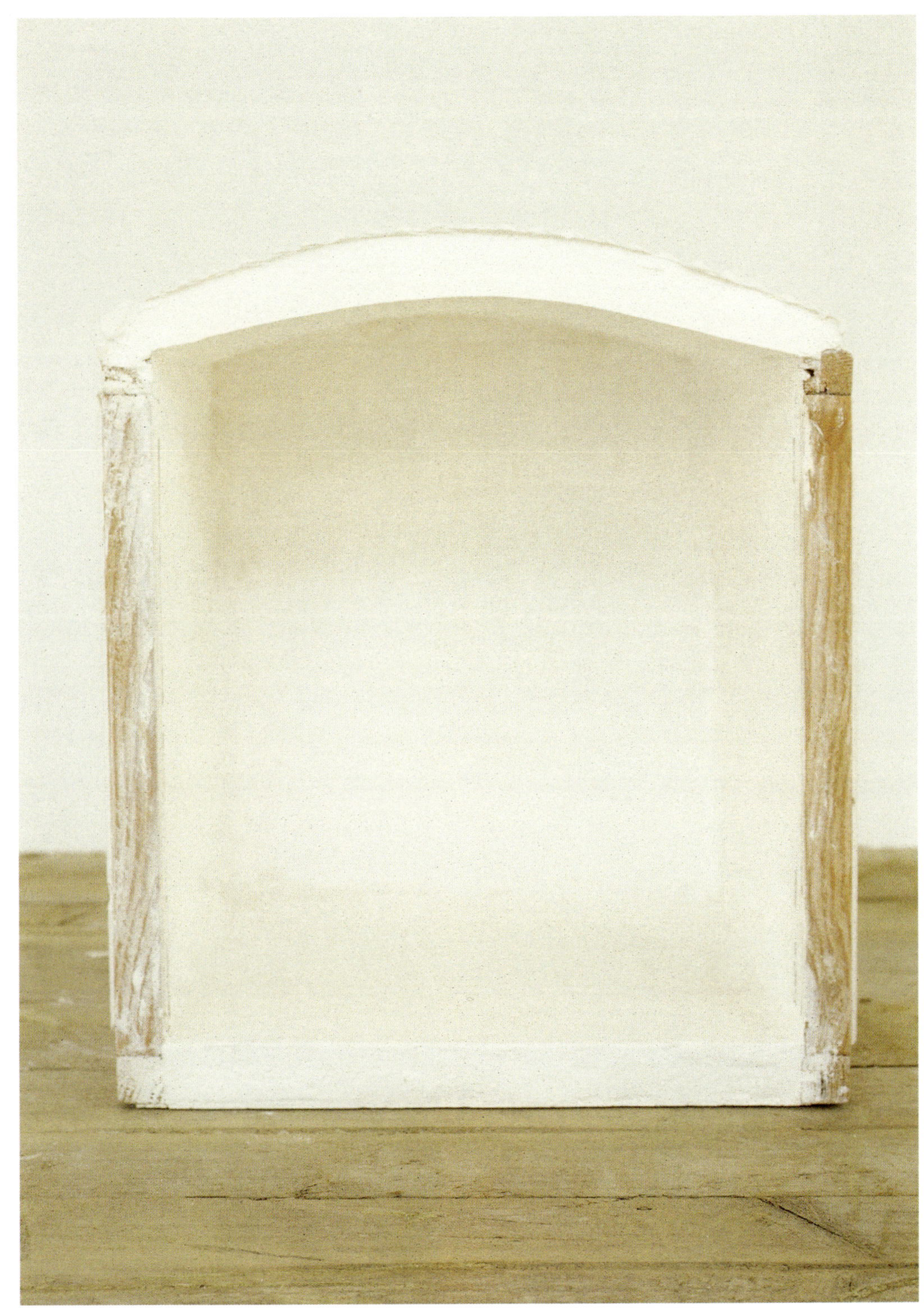

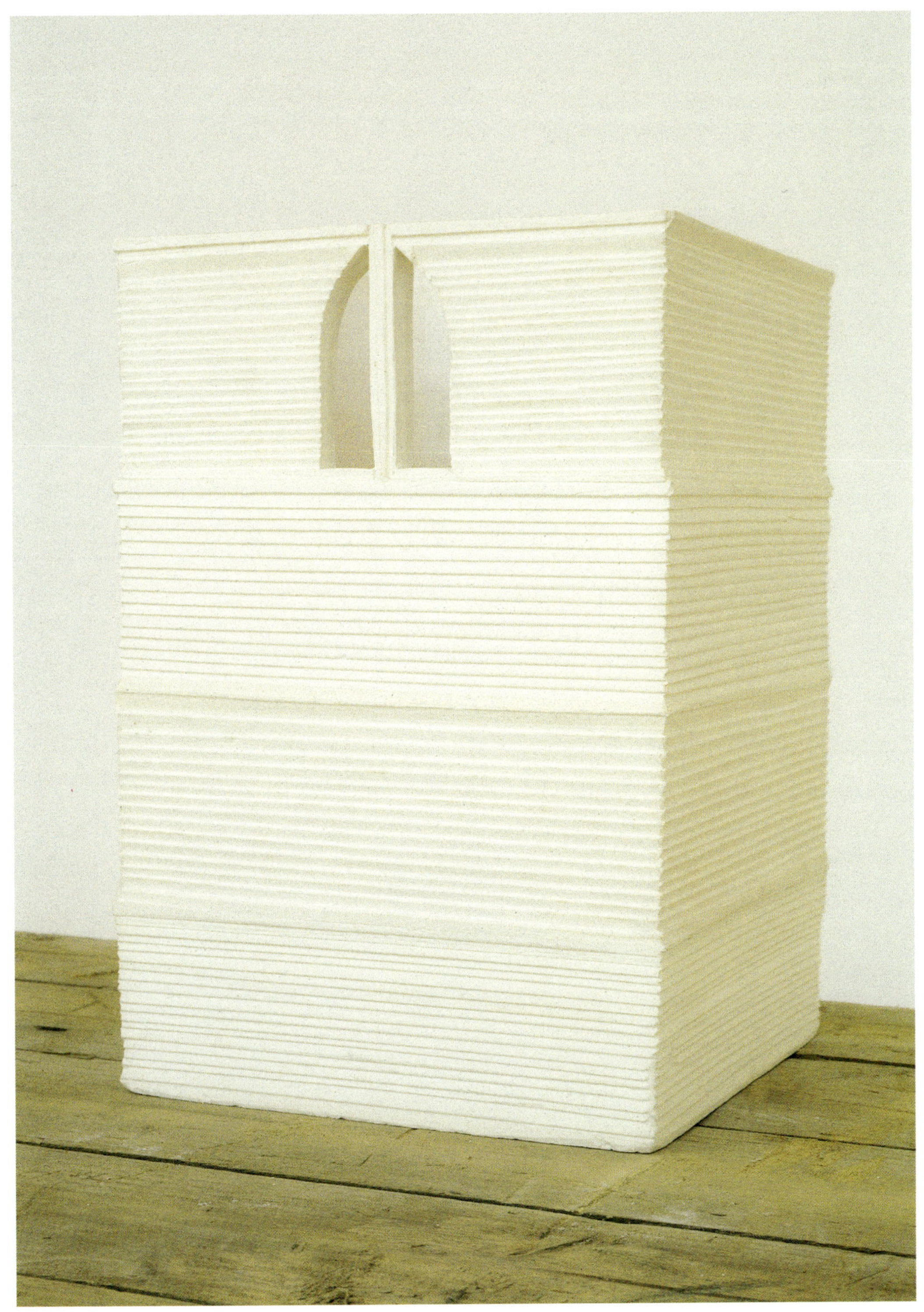

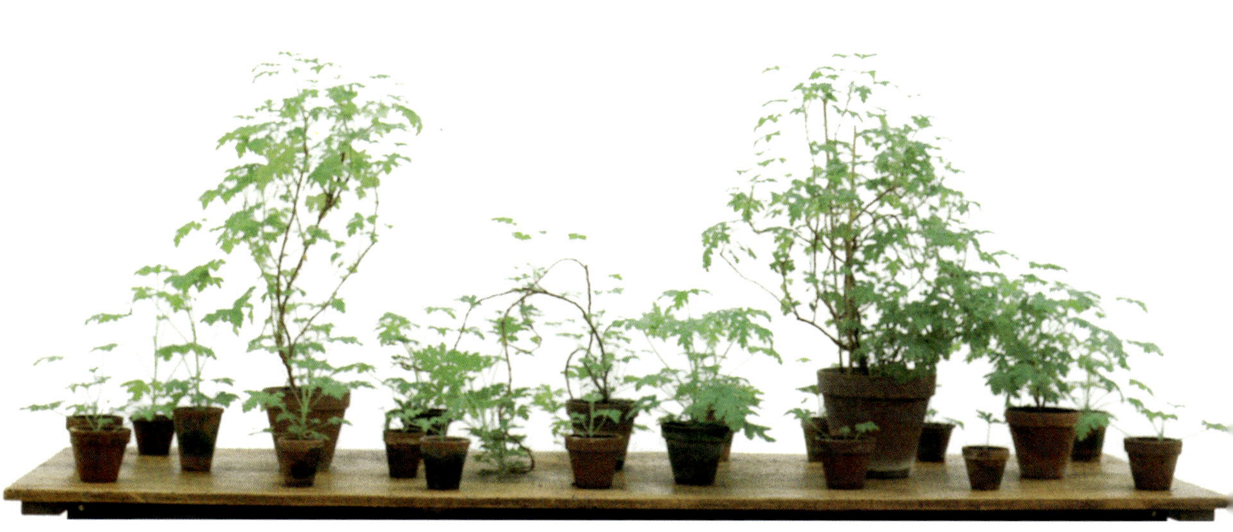

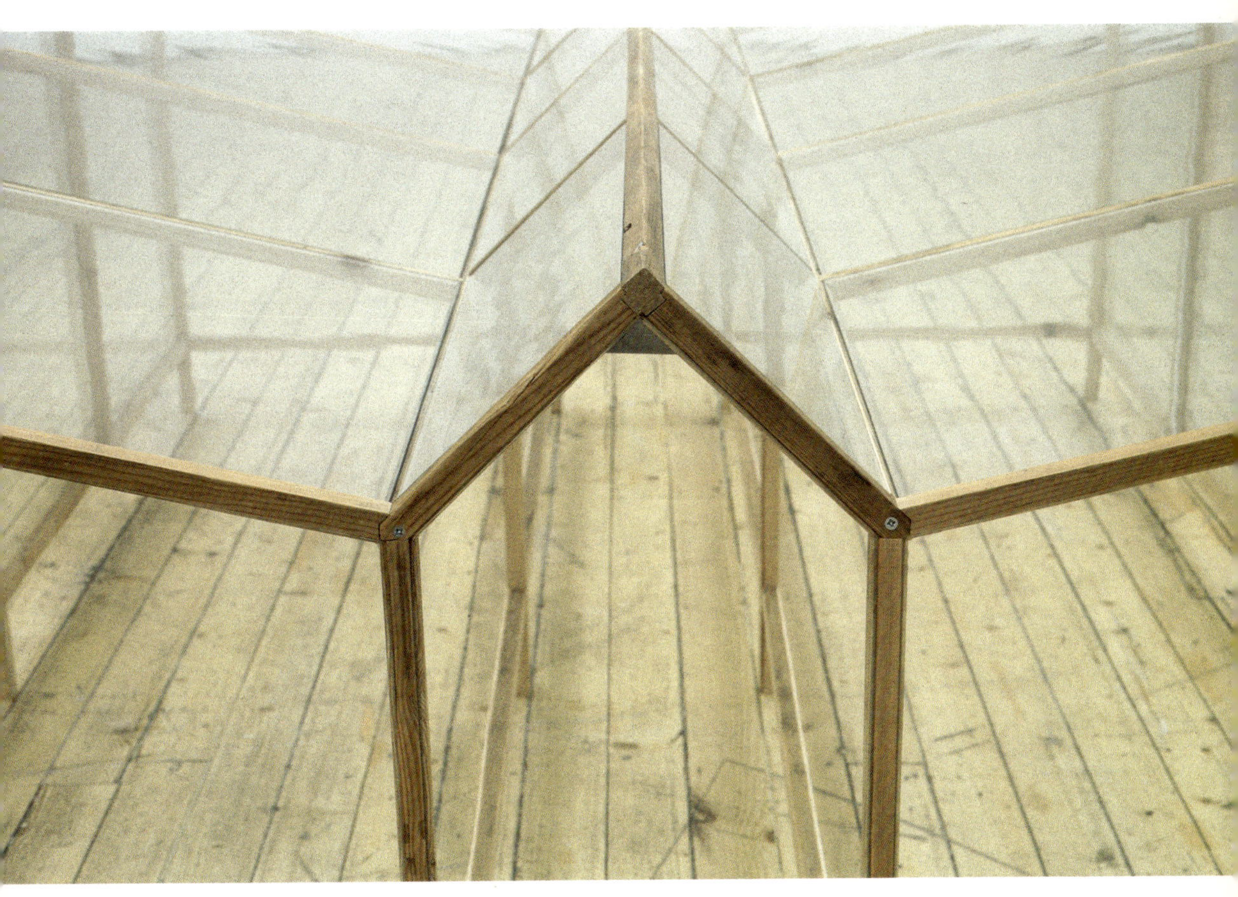

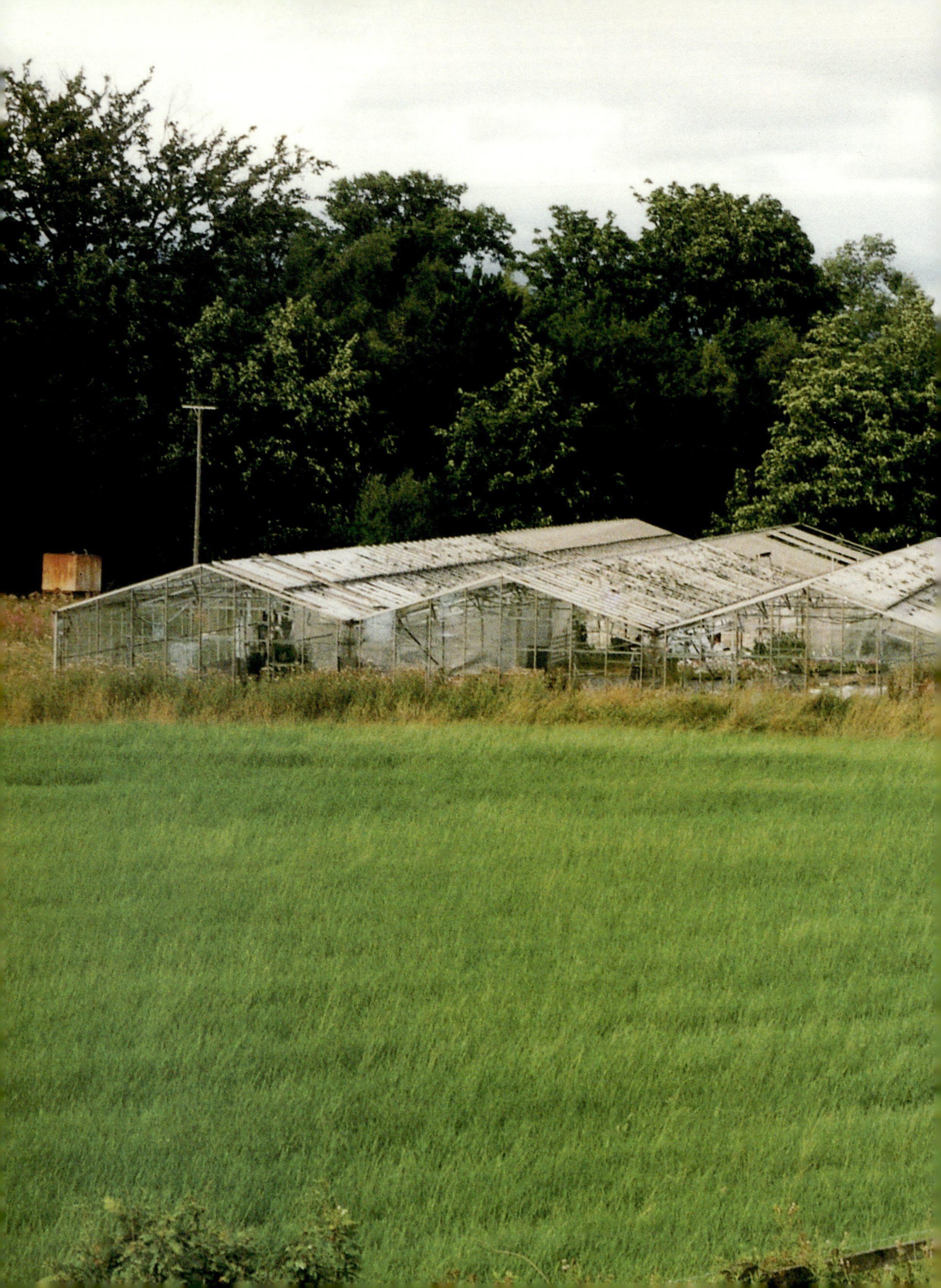

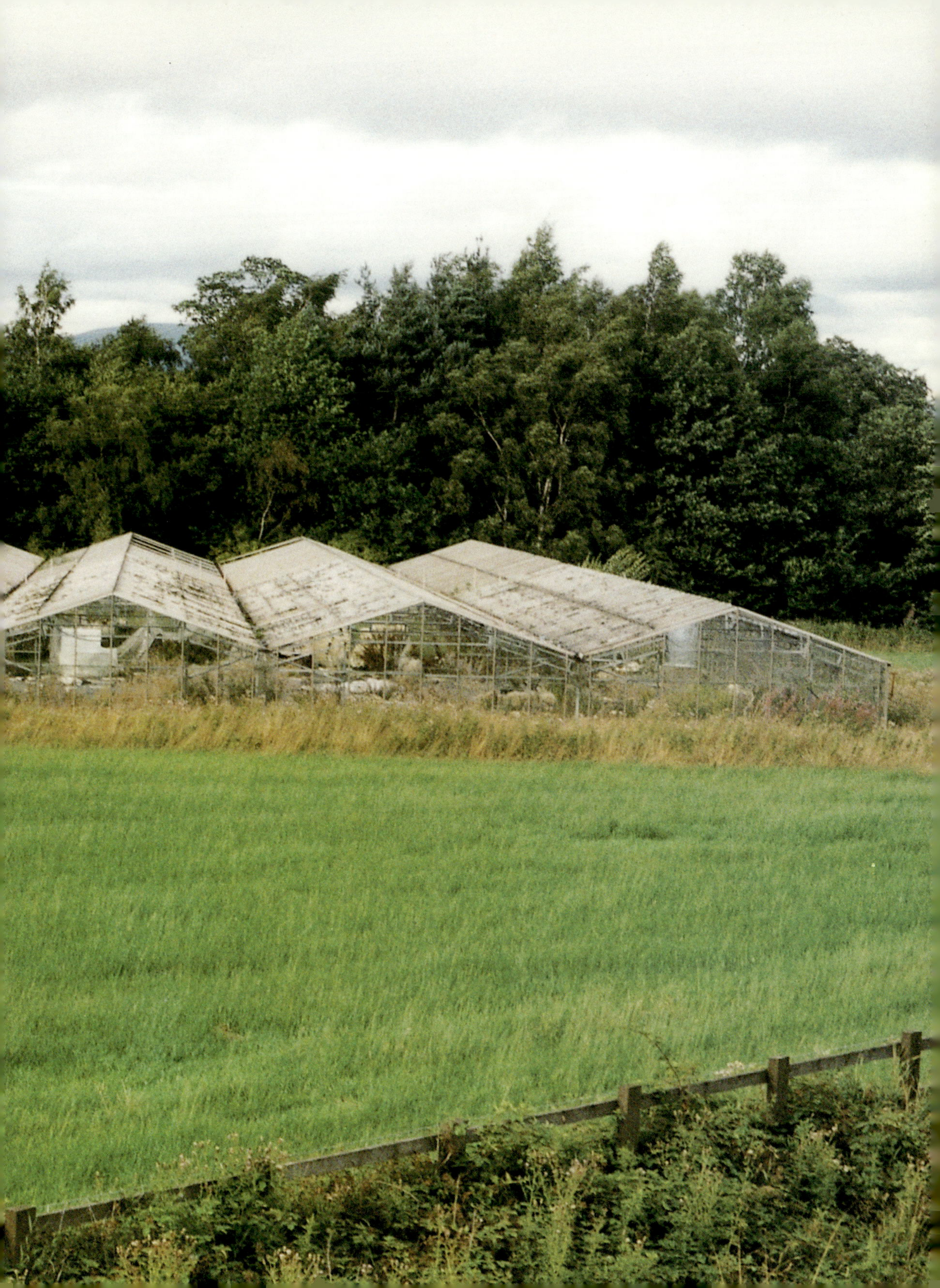

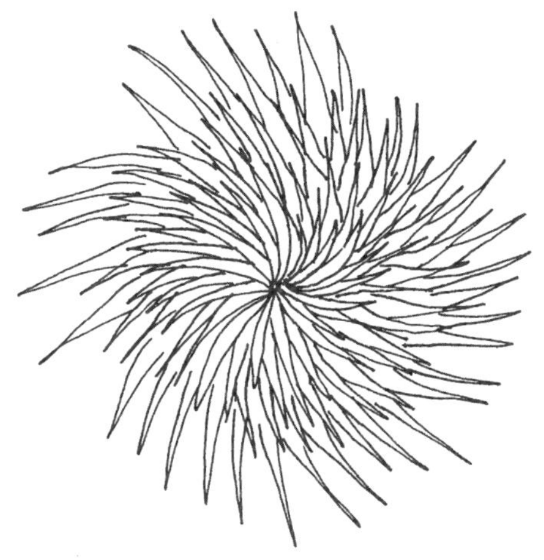

Essay

by John Calcutt

There is an art that points – tediously, redundantly – to the world as it has become: today.

Fascinated or repelled, it remains nonetheless enslaved. Mesmerised in a mirrored cell, it finds no way beyond the guarding force of the present. If it summons a past, it is often a recent past, one enclosed by the perimeter walls of personal memory. If it hails a future, it is a future enthralled by the tyranny of currently installed laws. There is another art, however, that finds freedom, escaping to a clear space of contemplation. It is as if an extra set of dimensions has been discovered, dimensions within and beyond those of the present. Here lives the poetic force that animates mere existence with the resonance of being.

Already this appears impossibly romantic, implausibly idealist, stupidly inflated. And yet, I want to suggest that in the recent work of Annette Heyer we can follow the movement of such an escape: a movement, moreover, with power and grace enough to defeat such accusations. But to appreciate the liberating experience this work offers we must be prepared to immerse ourselves in a kind of attentive reverie, attuning ourselves to subtleties and nuances whose modest appearances conceal unimagined possibilities. Lost meaning inhabits the slightest inflection of forms. While each of Heyer's individual works retains its own integrity, it is also the passages between them – their respective spacings and placings – that set their operations in motion. In The Fruitmarket Gallery they guide the movements of our bodies and our minds.

Double-back to the left at the top of the stairs. The materials of *Geraniums* (p. 33) are simply itemised: oak working table, flower pots, lemon geraniums. The work, however, stages an unexpected encounter. We are unaccustomed to the presence of living, organic matter in an art gallery. Is the function of these geraniums purely formal – to counter the sharp angularity of architectural geometry with floral arabesque and perfumed exhalation? Or are we to read them as symbolically loaded – as representatives of an uncontaminated nature thrown into dialectical

confrontation with the disciplining apparatus of culture? It is too soon to tell.
All we have are clues: the positioning of the work at the entrance to the exhibition;
the simple construction of the oak table; the unadorned functionalism of the
plant pots; the relative bareness of the display, its direct matter-of-factness.
And the presence of soil. Confined though it may be to plant pots on a plain
table, earth is nonetheless displayed on a rudimentary pedestal. Its earlier
absence from the list of *Geranium's* materials may be a simple oversight – or
it may suggest something more bewildering. Perhaps earth is not to be
understood as a material.

Pivot through ninety degrees clockwise, to view the long, north wall that
faces *Geraniums*. Imperceptibly, before any individual items are registered,
one is conscious of this wall and the objects it supports as a strong gestalt.
In an unadorned state the wall would be a blank, undefined field, present only
as vertical and lateral extension. Once 'occupied', however, the wall enters into
a dynamic relationship with its temporary 'contents'. Formerly a zone of
undefined potential, the wall now assumes the positive identity of a ground.
In this respect, the relation between wall and displayed object is similar to that
holding between a sheet of paper and the graphic marks it bears (be they
linguistic or pictorial). In all these instances there is a double movement.
The ground cannot be a ground without something to support (a 'figure'): the
figure cannot exist as a figure without some form of ground. Each brings the
other into existence. The nature of their relation, however, is dynamic and
unstable, varying as it does, from case to case.

In The Fruitmarket Gallery, Heyer converts the wall into a ground by
mounting *Concrete Cast* (p. 32) upon it. *Concrete Cast* divides the wall,
converting its undifferentiated field into an articulated ground. By virtue of
the double movement, this articulated ground provides the conditions for
Concrete Cast to perform its own act of articulation. If this explanation seems
unnecessarily abstruse, I will attempt to justify it. First: *Concrete Cast's* minimal
occupation of the ground it claims from the wall seems expressly to draw our
attention to the nature of their relation. Second: in considering the nature of
this relation we may begin to develop our understanding of Heyer's work. We
find ourselves drawn into speculation.

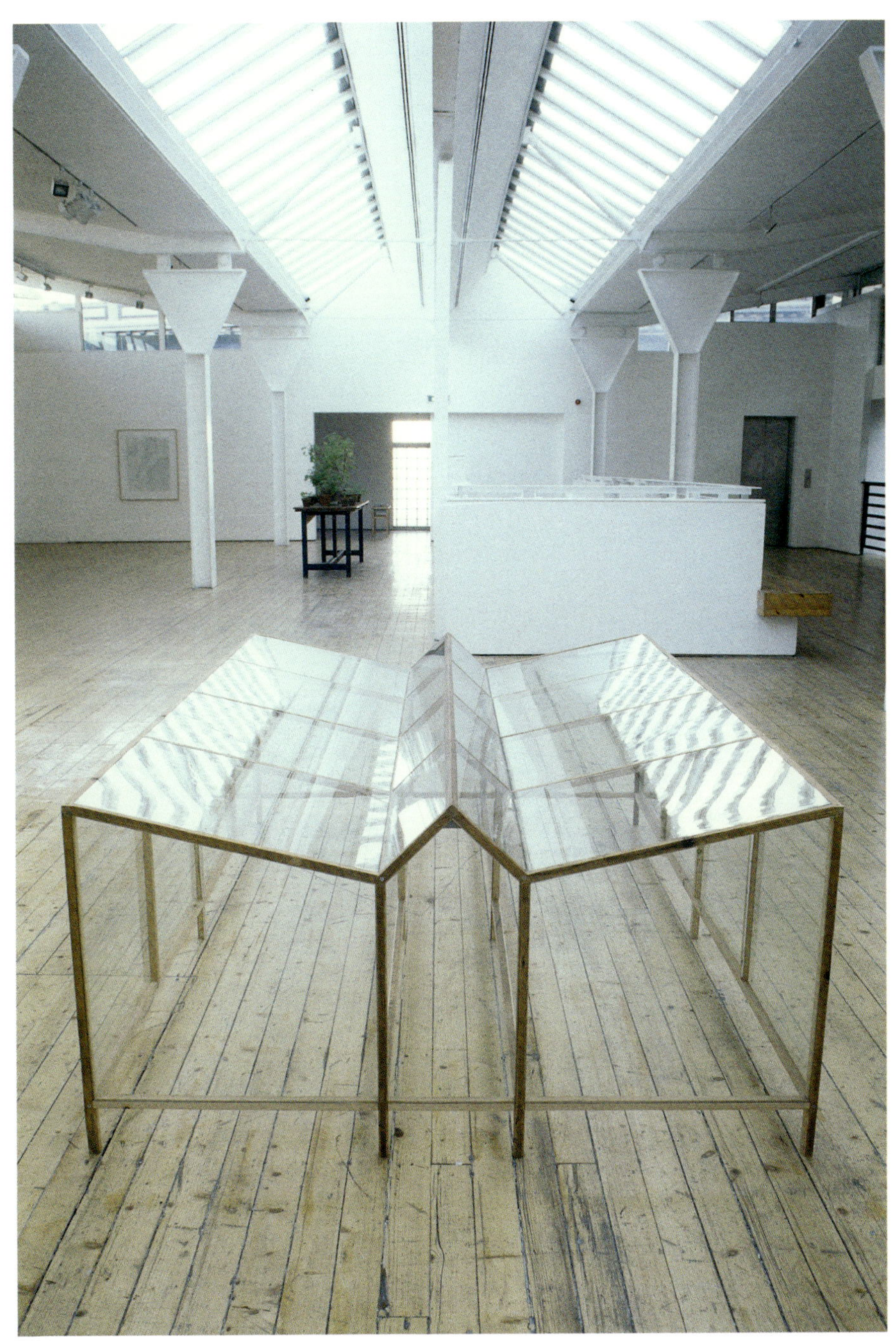

What is the nature of our being on this earth, under this sky? How do we
come into being as a consequence of our relation to these givens? Such primordial
questions are the stuff of philosophy but, unless grounded, they remain drifting and
pointless. Heyer's work, it seems to me, provides such a grounding. It offers an
embodiment of those very relations that philosophers (such as Martin Heidegger)
have attempted to conceptualise by other means. But if I refer to aspects of
Heidegger's work in the following, it is not to suggest that Heyer's work operates
in its shadow, or that it performs a secondary, illustrational task. Quite the contrary.
It is an attempt to reverse this relation, to suggest that Heyer's art is a site that
reveals philosophical thought as probable and viable.

Thus, there is something in Heidegger's characterisation of the exchange
between earth and world which is validated by that exchange between ground
and figure staged in *Concrete Cast*. In a bid to secure his speculation, Heidegger
resorts to an architectural image, a temple built on a rocky outcrop.

> *"Standing there, the building rests on the rocky ground. This resting*
> *of the work draws up out of the rock the mystery of that rock's clumsy*
> *yet spontaneous support.… The lustre and gleam of the stone, though*
> *itself apparently glowing only by the grace of the sun, yet first brings*
> *to light the light of the day, the breadth of the sky, the darkness of the*
> *night. The temple's firm towering makes visible the invisible space of*
> *air.… Tree and grass, eagle and bull, snake and cricket first enter into*
> *their distinctive shapes and thus come to appear as what they are. The*
> *Greeks early called this emerging and rising in all things 'physis'. It*
> *clears and illuminates, also, that on and in which man bases his*
> *dwelling. We call this ground the 'earth'."* [†]

In the light of this image, it is not without significance, perhaps, that the
forms of Heyer's *Concrete Cast* themselves suggest the elements of a rudimentary
architectural vocabulary. They evoke brackets, vaults and buttresses, but they
are like early utterances in a language still to be developed and refined. They
strive towards articulate expressions of supporting and bracing, but remain
close to isolated, disjointed fragments of speech. Articulateness depends upon
differentiation: the greater the degree of differentiation, the greater the degree

of articulation. *Concrete Cast* operates at a low level of differentiation, and yet this careful management of difference guarantees it as a primary thematic element of the work. Thus the work's title suggests a single item, and yet it comprises two distinctly separate physical units. Each of these units is itself composed of two clearly combined components (upper and lower). All four components share the same basic form, although the upper components are arranged in such a way as to 'mirror' the lower. The components derive their form from the intersection of two primary geometrical figures: the rectangle and the arc. Each component is inscribed with a different decorative motif (all these motifs being elementary variations upon basic geometric forms: parallel lines, diamond and lozenge patterns, or chevrons). One of the components remains clamped in a wooden brace. These few sentences virtually exhaust the catalogue of differences operational throughout the work, but they do not begin to account for their significance.

To claim that meaning is dependent upon a relation of difference (that earth and world, for example, come into being as a result of a mutually defining play of otherness) is only partially satisfactory as an explanation. It fails to address the reciprocal dynamism characterising that relation of difference. Thus for Heidegger, for example, the world is concerned with investigation, discovery, questioning. It seeks to understand the earth, to impose meanings upon it, to derive resources from it. Conversely, the earth (which is *"not to be associated with the idea of a mass of matter deposited somewhere"*) is *"sheltering and concealing"*. It resists the world's intrusions by retreating into the realm of the unknowable (hence, perhaps, the unnameable aspect of *Geranium's* soil). There is thus a conflict between the *"self-opening"* of world and the concealment of earth. Each, however, relies upon the other. It is at this point that the work of art finds its vocation: its task being to somehow negotiate between the two, helping the world to develop its articulate self and allowing the earth to be its mute self.

Already there is a strong sense that this is what Heyer's work does. Between plants and soil and primitive architectural elements, it occupies a mobile space in which the conflict between earth and world (often under the formal guise of a ground/figure dichotomy, and the metaphorical guise of a nature/culture dichotomy) is kept to a minimum. The strictly controlled play of difference in *Concrete Cast* – both in terms of its relation to the wall/ground and in terms of

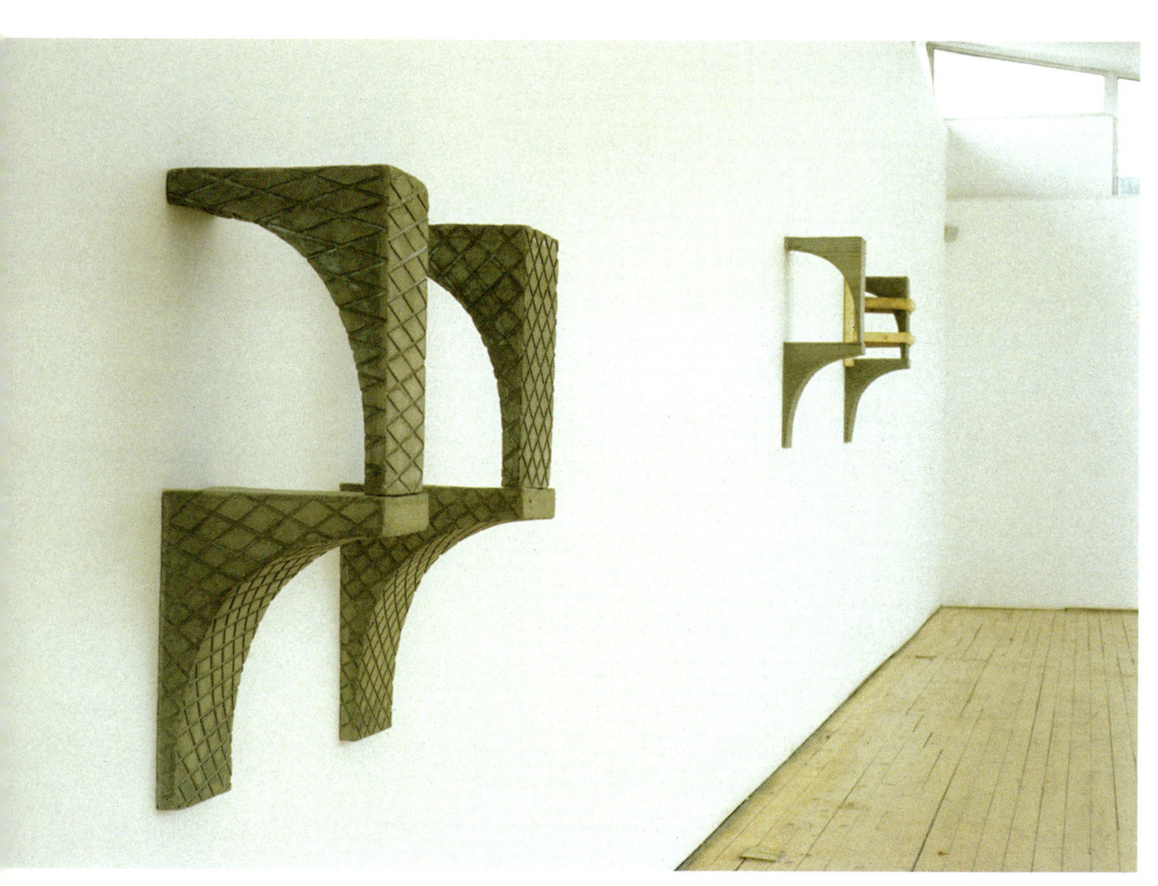

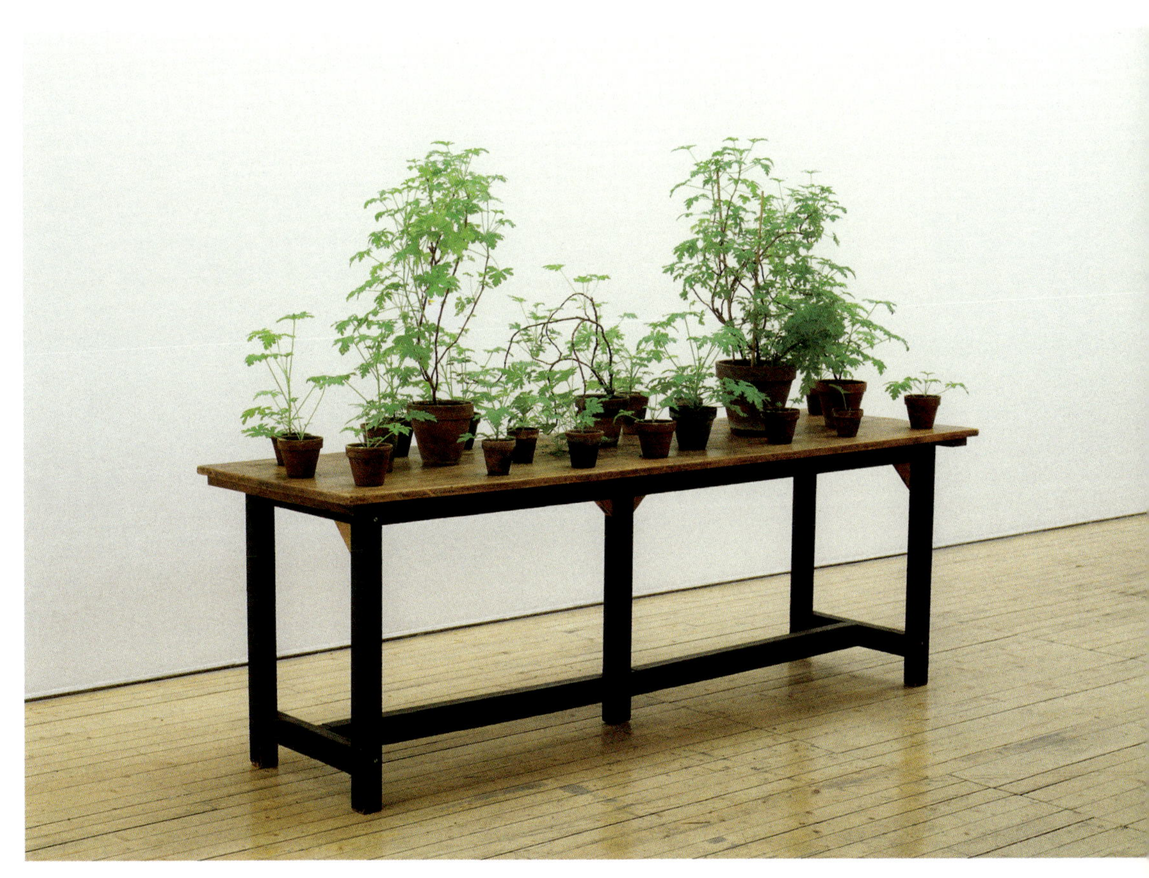

the internal relations of its constituent elements – might now be seen as symptomatic of a desire to achieve a measure of equilibrium between these competing demands. To bring into being and let be, so to speak.

Turn left towards the west wall. Placed directly on the floor and surrounded by circulating space is an object constructed from Douglas Fir and greenhouse glass. Its architectural character is confirmed by its title: *Glasshouse* (p. 29). The central axis of the structure is aligned exactly with that of the gallery. Its glass roof echoes (but does not replicate) the glazed skylights that run the length of the gallery. Just as the temple resting on its rocky ground draws out the visibility of its immediate environment, so *Glasshouse* develops our awareness of those spaces it reflects and refracts, extends and curtails. Unlike *Concrete Cast*, however, *Glasshouse* provides a model of a completely enclosing architectural space. It offers a complete architectural statement rather than disconnected phrases of scattered nouns and adjectives. And yet it shares *Concrete Cast*'s reluctant stance towards strong differentiation. Its walls and roof are transparent, offering the weakest frontiers between the space it defines and the space it occupies. It is there, but barely. Its inside scarcely displaces its outside, while its outside appears to flow freely through its interior. It *"makes space for… spaciousness;"* its task is to *"liberate the free space of the open region"* and *"hold open the open region of the world"*.

It is a work that, in the context of The Fruitmarket Gallery exhibition, points in several directions beyond itself even as its own physicality recedes. The temple causes the rock *"to come forth for the very first time"*. It draws the rock into the world. At the same time, however, the temple *"sets itself back"* into the materials from which it is made: in other words, into the earth. In its manner of occupying and echoing, *Glasshouse* virtually forces us to 'see' the architecture of the gallery anew. The white cube ceases to be a neutral container and is reanimated as an active participant. We cannot ignore its spatial imposition, the world created by its act of enclosure. Space is, by and large, something that we take for granted. It is often thought of, in fact, as some thing. We easily believe that it is always and ever available to be measured, and thus captured, defined and known. *Glasshouse* begins to make us doubt such easy certainty. Meanwhile, the nature of *Glasshouse* is subject to a supplementary process of refinement.

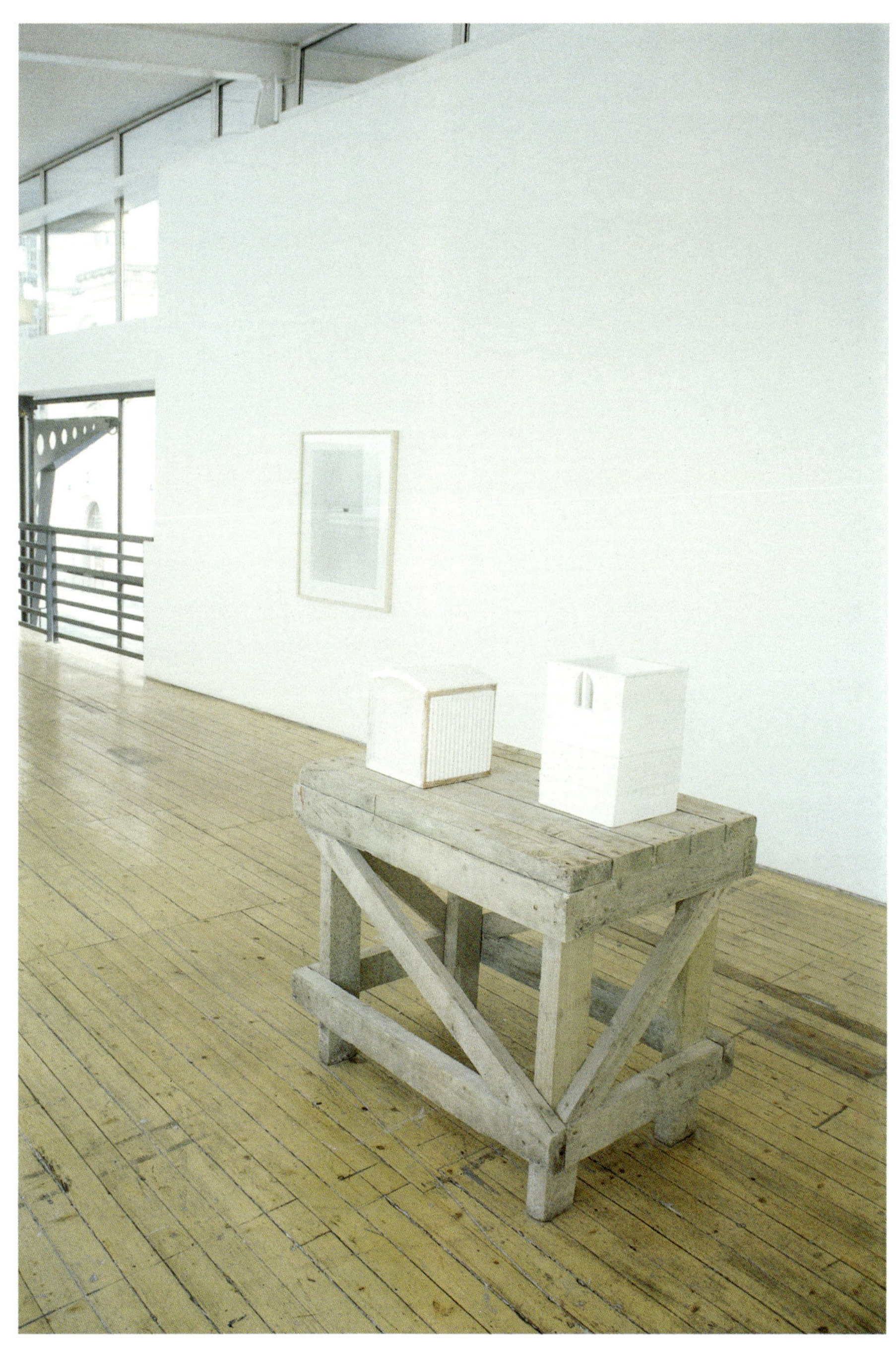

Recall. The fact that this *Glasshouse* is also a greenhouse refers us back to
Geraniums. Plants have no world. They exercise no conscious exchange with
the earth. Only when brought into the orbit of human cultivation do they enter
a world. *Geraniums*, therefore, enters into a spatial and temporal dialogue with
Glasshouse. But we must not overlook the purely conceptual aspect of their
relation. *Glasshouse* may signify a greenhouse, but it does not function as one.
It contains no plants. As such, it remains useless. Its distance from the demands
of practical usage – its failure as a piece of utilitarian equipment – guarantees its
status as a work of art capable of making and securing *"space for… spaciousness"*.

Geraniums grow upwards from the earth, straining towards the light from
above. The transparent roof of the *Glasshouse* is ready to welcome the sky into
the open spaces it shelters. What is the sky? It is the primordial source of all
measurement – a measurement far greater and more profound than that offered
by standardised systems of calibration. The vaulting range of the sky absorbs
the breadth and depth of vision: its rhythms of darkness and light are inexorable
and perpetual. Nothing exceeds the span and scope of its tall distance. The
face of the sky, wrote Hölderlin, is full of the qualities of an unknown God.
In acknowledging the enveloping gaze of the sky, humanity is affirmed of its
existence on earth. We exist, says Heidegger, within the fourfold: earth and
mortals, sky and divinities.

To the south wall. There are framed photographs that we have so far overlooked,
but we will return to them in due course. The immediate object of our attention
here is a sturdy, inelegant, pine stone-cutter's table surmounted by two small
box-like structures fabricated from plaster and pine. The work is entitled *Shelter*
(p. 35). Unlike *Glasshouse*, the structure that forms the largest physical aspect of
Shelter – the pine stone-cutter's table – retains its equipmental identity. That is not
to say, however, that this identity is unmodified. Normally a base on which things
are made – at which tools are deployed – it now serves temporarily as a base on
which things are displayed. A trivial shift, perhaps, but, like all aspects of Heyer's
work, one which may signal a fundamental reorientation. The movement from
doing to looking, from making to contemplating, has considerable implications.
Marooned in a gallery, the pine stone-cutter's table speaks of an absence: the
absence of a working relationship with tools. This working relationship is itself a

mode of addressing ourselves to the world (and consequently to the earth).
When working-with is displaced by looking-at the world recedes into dubious
abstraction.

Dwell. Placed on the workbench are two white plaster objects. They seem
to be models of buildings but, like *Concrete Cast*, they remain incomplete as
architectural statements. Even if built to full scale, these models would not
provide adequate spaces in which to live, work or worship. They abstract and
reduce the habitable essence of architecture to the point of its extinction. Or,
more precisely, they strip building of its functional aspect, its utilitarian practicality.
What remains, however, is a purified sense of building as a space cleared for
dwelling. But what is dwelling? Dwelling, according once more to Heidegger,
is the fundamental state of our being on earth. Dwelling, he claims, is being.
On the one hand, it is not *"merely the occupying of a lodging"*. Dwelling is
being, and dwelling is building. We build because we dwell. By means of building,
humanity makes spaces in which the interplay of the fourfold (earth and sky,
mortals and divinities) may be made manifest. By means of building (which
takes two forms; the cultivation of growing things and the erecting of edifices),
humanity demonstrates its care for the world.

The essence of building is thus revealed as a means of situating humanity.
Before it is a house or a temple or a factory or a prison, a building is a primal
assertion of dwelling on the earth with fellow mortals beneath a sky that bears
the gaze of divinities.

To build is to create space and to organise the relation between humanity
and space. But our everyday understanding of space needs to be suspended
here. This is not a mathematical or geometrical space; it is a space whose measure
is wrested from the sky by poets. *"The radiance of its height is itself the darkness
of its all-sheltering breadth. The blue of the sky's lovely blueness is the colour
of depth. The radiance of the sky is the dawn and dusk of the twilight, which
shelters everything that can be proclaimed. This sky is the measure."* It is not a
measurable and quantifiable space that surrounds or faces us: *"It is* [like the spaces
of *Glasshouse*] *neither an external object nor an inner experience."* As much as we
create space, we are created by space. All of these possibilities can be suggested
by *Shelter*, suggested because it is a work that finally asserts space as a meaningful

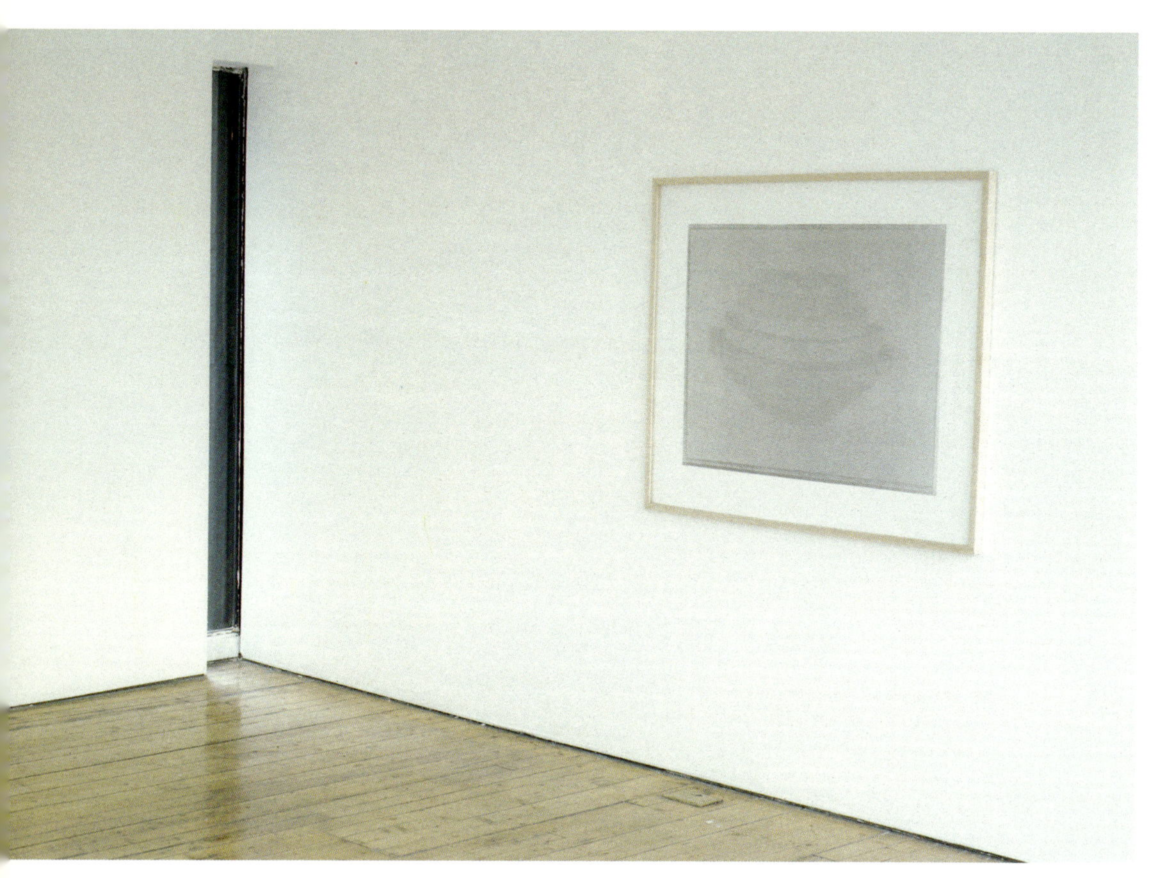

material in Heyer's work. This is not simply the localised spaces that the individual items articulate by means of their occupation, enclosure and extension, but the spaces that separate and unite them in a unified field of spaciousness.

Approach. As I write I re-enter the spaces cleared and installed by the exhibition. Even from a distance I feel close. Close enough to reflect again on the ways in which the spaces and distances between the various works in the exhibition set in motion a relay of traces, echoes, anticipations and recollections. *Concrete Cast* helped me to understand *Geraniums*, just as it prepared me for *Glasshouse*. My body stands in front of *Shelter* while my mind has already returned to *Geraniums*: *"in going through spaces we do not give up our standing in them. Rather, we always go through spaces in such a way that we already experience them by staying constantly with near and remote locations and things.... I am never only here, as this encapsulated body; rather, I am there, that is, I already pervade the room, and only thus can I go through it."*

At some point in these walking tours (the real tour, the remembered tour, this written tour) we pass into and through new spaces. These spaces are simultaneously real and imaginary; precisely measurable and measurable only with the resources of contemplative reverie. They are spaces that accommodate the present and the past, hereness and thereness. They are the resonant spaces opened and inhabited by Heyer's work. They are also fragile and provisional. They exist only and for as long as we choose to recognise their possibilities and inhabit them.

Wander. On the wall behind *Shelter* are two framed images; *Corridor* (p. 14) to the right, *Staircase* (p. 13) to the left. Along with *Cerberus* (on the west wall, to the left of *Glasshouse*, close to the corner formed by the south wall, p. 15, 38) and *Corner* (on the shorter east wall, close to the corner formed by the north wall, p. 17) they play the exhibition's spatial themes in two dimensions. But they are immediately ambiguous: are they photographs or prints (lithographs, perhaps), hand-made or mechanically produced? Their motifs suggest architectural forms, but it is not at all clear what these forms might be. *Corner* suggests a staircase, but its stepped forms begin in mid-air and terminate in a blank wall. The image entitled *Staircase* hints, with apparent perversity, at an architecture for animals or insects – a bird box or a bee hive – thereby indexing *Glasshouse's* architecture for plants and, consequently, the theme of humanity's realisation of dwelling through the cultivation of nature and through building structures

All four images are united, however, in certain common features. They all exhibit minimal tonal contrast and are pitched at the high, white end of the tonal spectrum. In that sense, they may be thought of as developing the thematic of low-level differentiation witnessed in the sculptural works. The nature of the depicted forms' emergence from their grounds would also seem to restate this fundamental process. The curving forms of *Corridor* and *Cerberus* swell from a flat, white surface as if continuous with that surface. In *Corner* and *Staircase* the identity of the forms is dependent upon the angle formed by the meeting of two planes. As with the temple on its rocky foundation, form and ground bring each other into sharper presence. The stepped, ziggurat-like structure, of all the forms in these silver gelatine prints, also draws our attention to that most elemental act of form-giving – the differentiation of the vertical from the horizontal.

Ultimately, however, these images prompt us to reflect upon a delicate economy of presence and absence, of being and not being. As photographs they already mark the spatial and temporal absence of those forms that once appeared before the camera's lens in another place. These pale, ghostly traces exist in marked contrast to the raw presence of *Shelter* and *Concrete Cast*, to their tangible forms and strongly tactile surfaces. Furthermore, we sense that these photographed forms might, in themselves, be taken from casts – plaster impressions of negative forms. They are reminders of the persistence of the concealed within the unconcealed, of the hidden within the manifest, of the overlooked and the forgotten within the considered and the remembered.

By the opening up of a world, all things gain their lingering and hastening, their remoteness and nearness, their scope and limits."

† All quotes from: *The Origin of the Work of Art*; *Building, Dwelling, Thinking*; *Poetically Man Dwells*, included in Martin Heidegger, *Poetry, Language, Thought*, trans. A. Hofstadter, New York, Harper & Row, 1971.

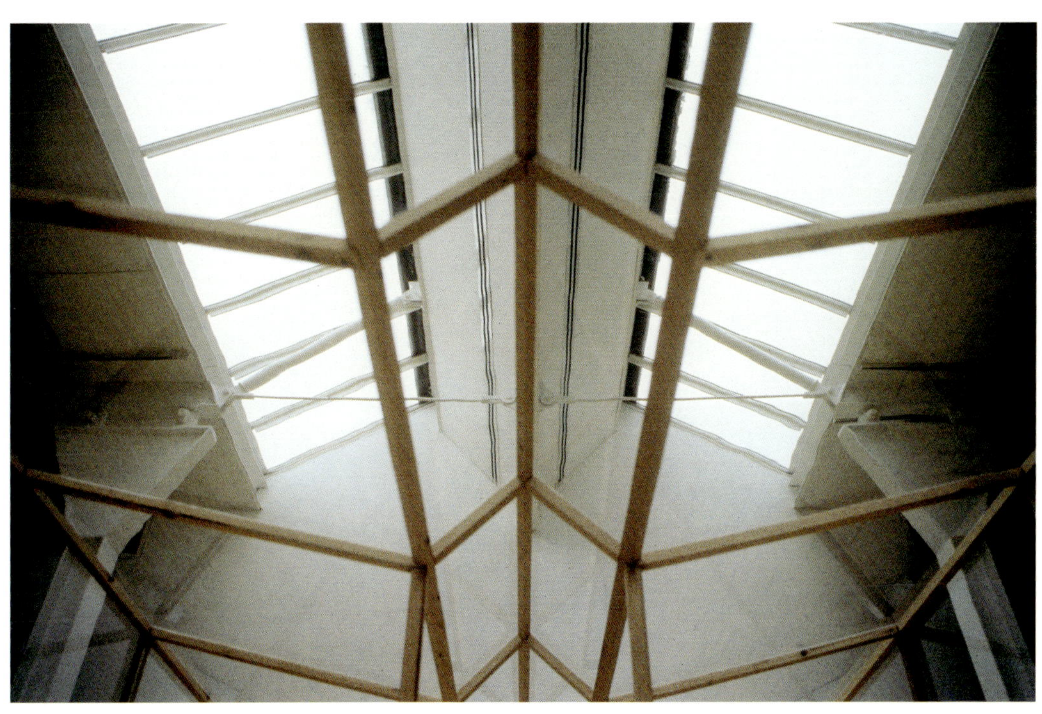

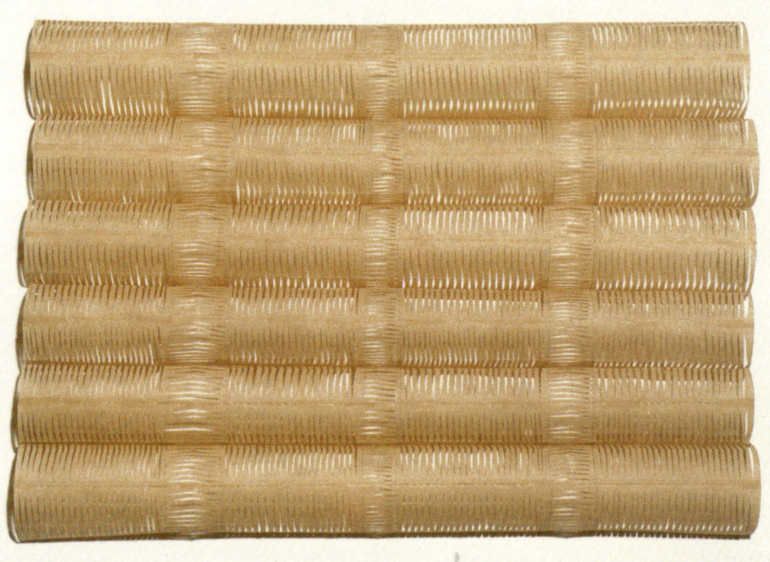

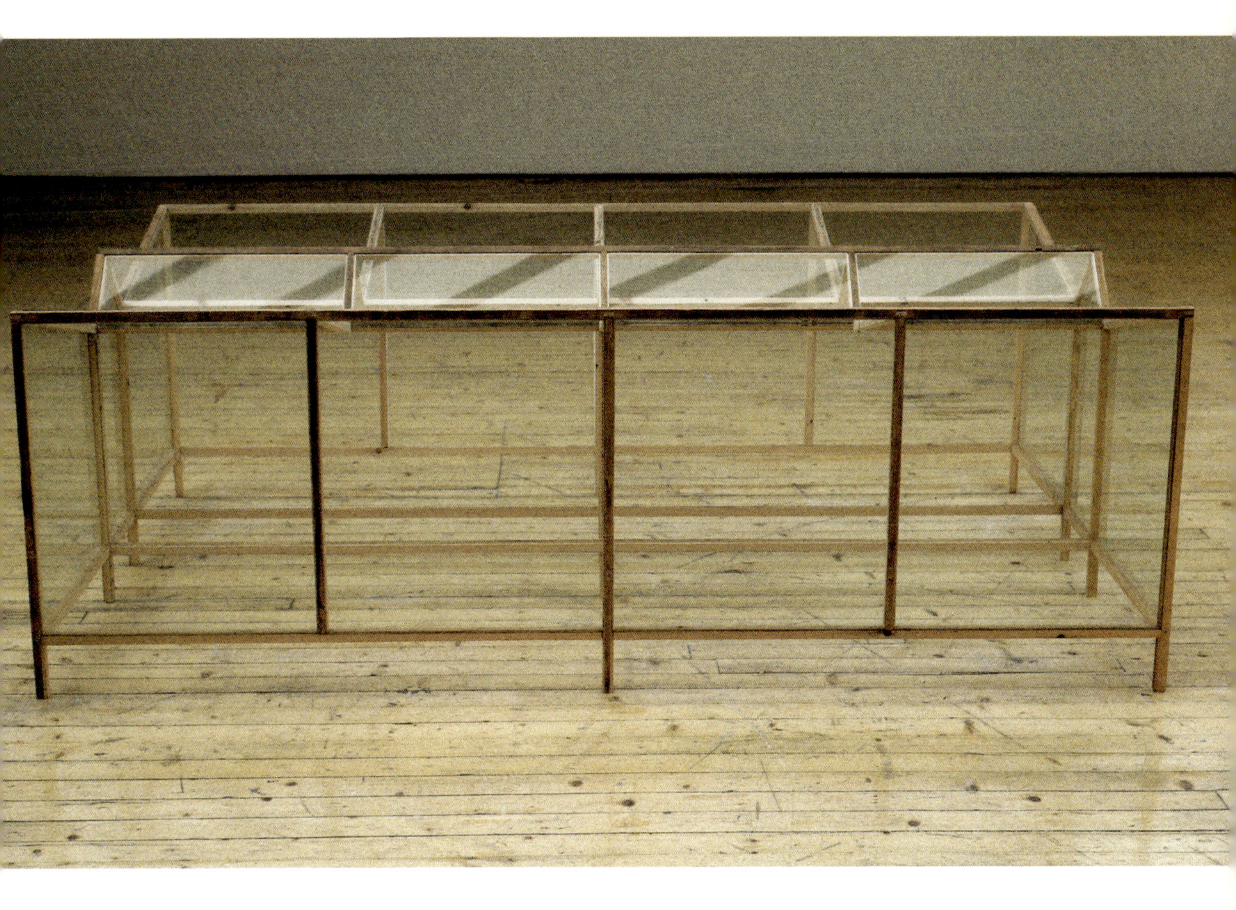

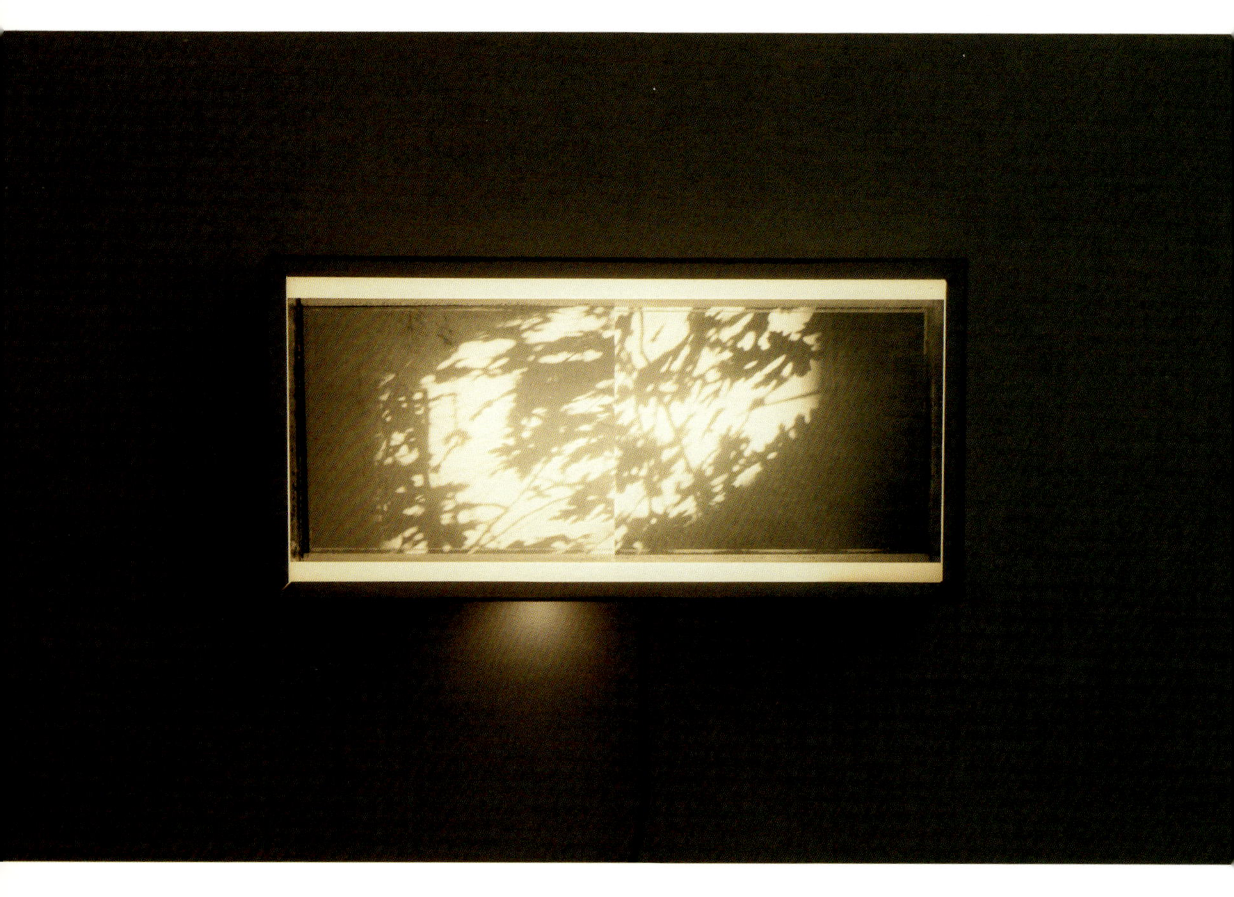

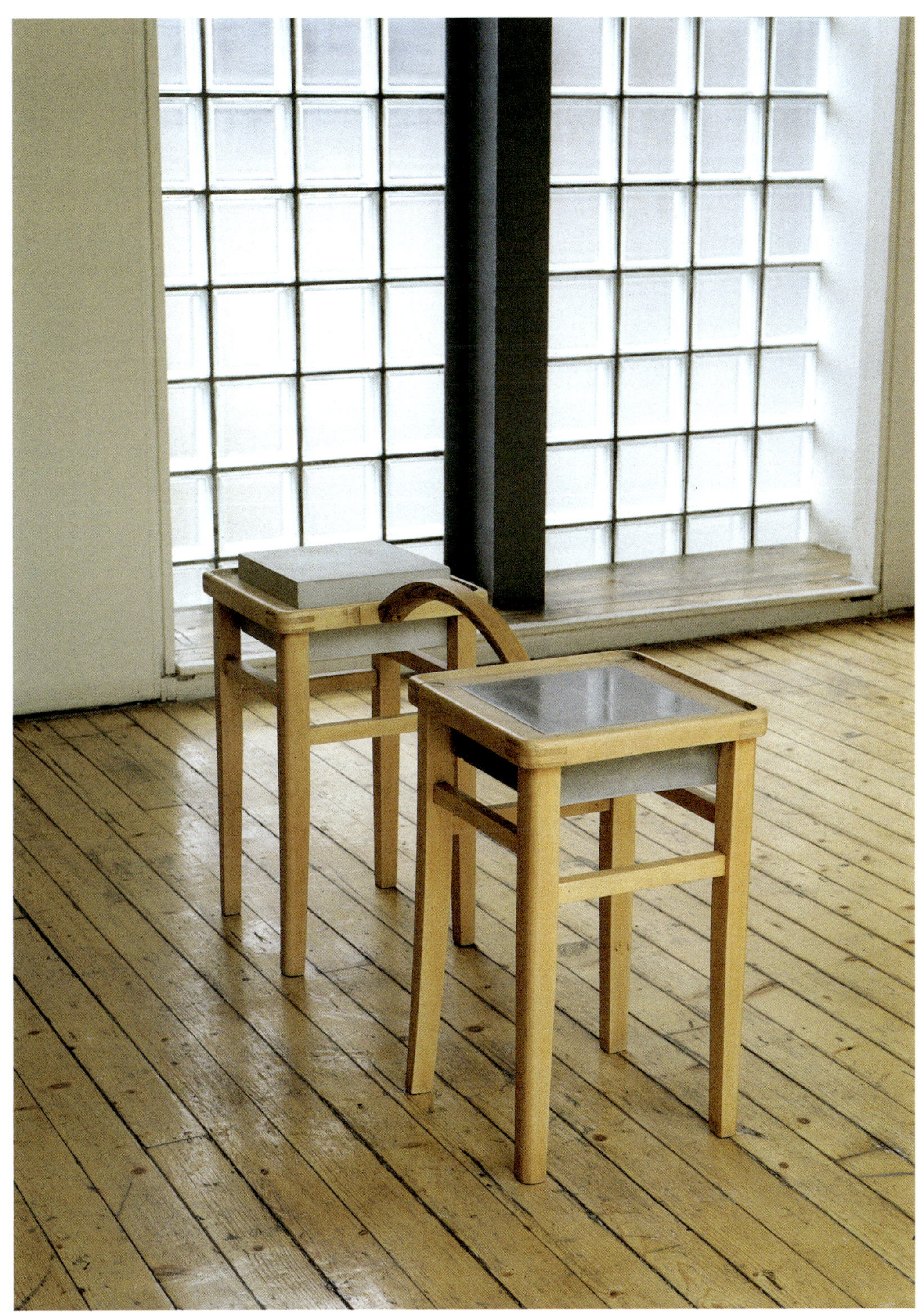

Excerpts from a Conversation

Franziska Bark & Annette Heyer

FB   Walking through your exhibition, I was struck by the rhythm in the positioning of the work and also by the transitoriness of one's relationship with the pieces in the space. Do you think in rhythmic terms?

AH   In a sense, yes. By placing the work in the gallery in this way, I was trying to initiate a kind of movement through the space. For example, *Concrete Cast* (pages 6, 7, 11, 32) was made through a drawing process, using pieces of cardboard to find a certain pattern and rhythm. A surface, a skin, is drawn that eventually becomes a three-dimensional object that is cast directly in the space. The elements of *Concrete Cast* maintain their reference to the drawing, though they're roughly formed from a building material into architectural fragments.

It's like in Giotto's fresco, *Driving the Demons from Arezzo*. The buildings appear independently to be moving from something two-dimensional into something three-dimensional. The construction of the city becomes organic and is very physical. The way it's painted doesn't allow for a singular perspective.

FB   Yes. The ambivalence of perspective is echoed by one's own movement and relationship to the objects. From a distance, they emphasise their two-dimensionality while, in proximity, they're very much spatial objects. This movement (from close up to far away and vice versa) operates throughout the exhibition even though the individual pieces have very different moods or qualities of temperature.

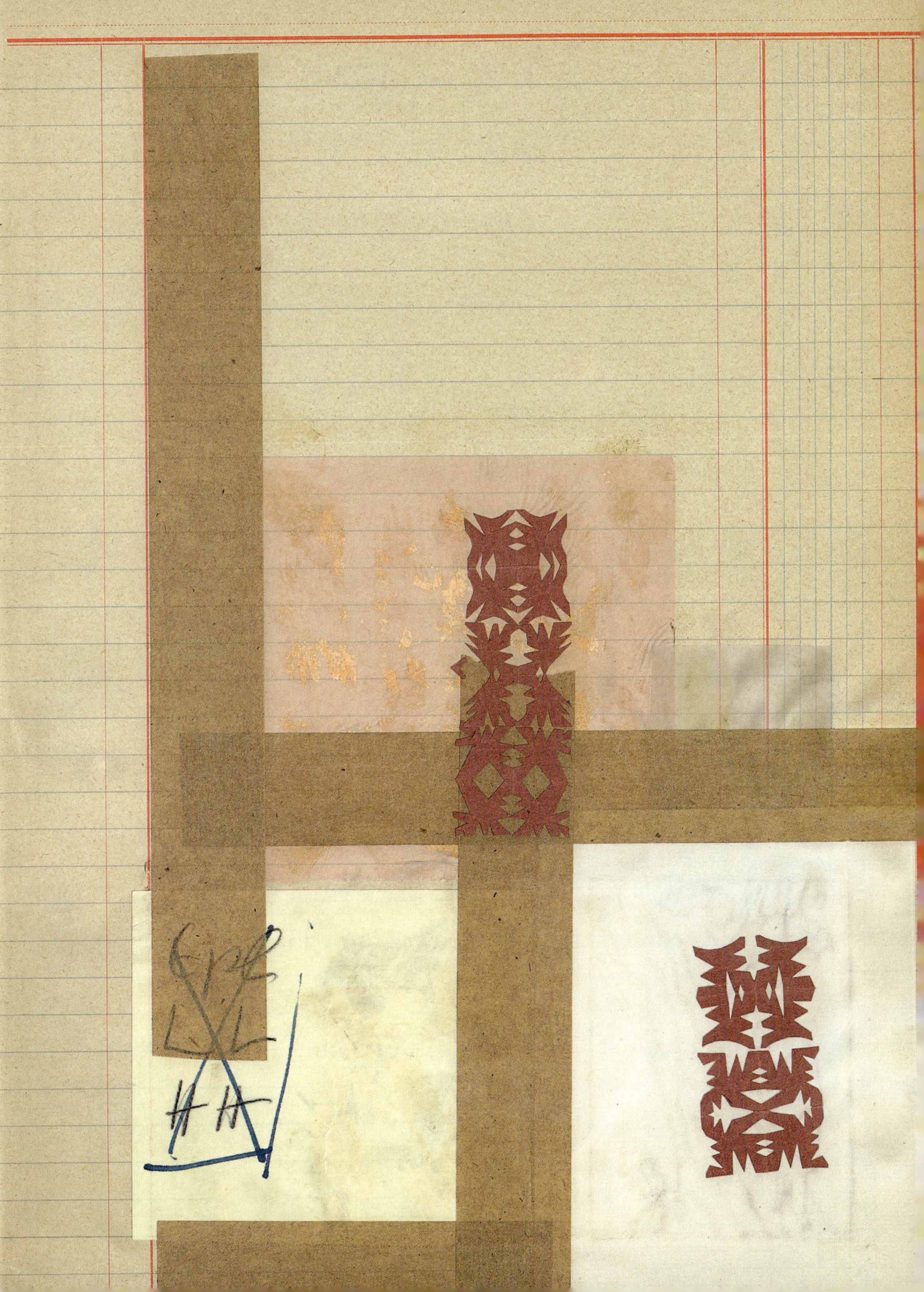

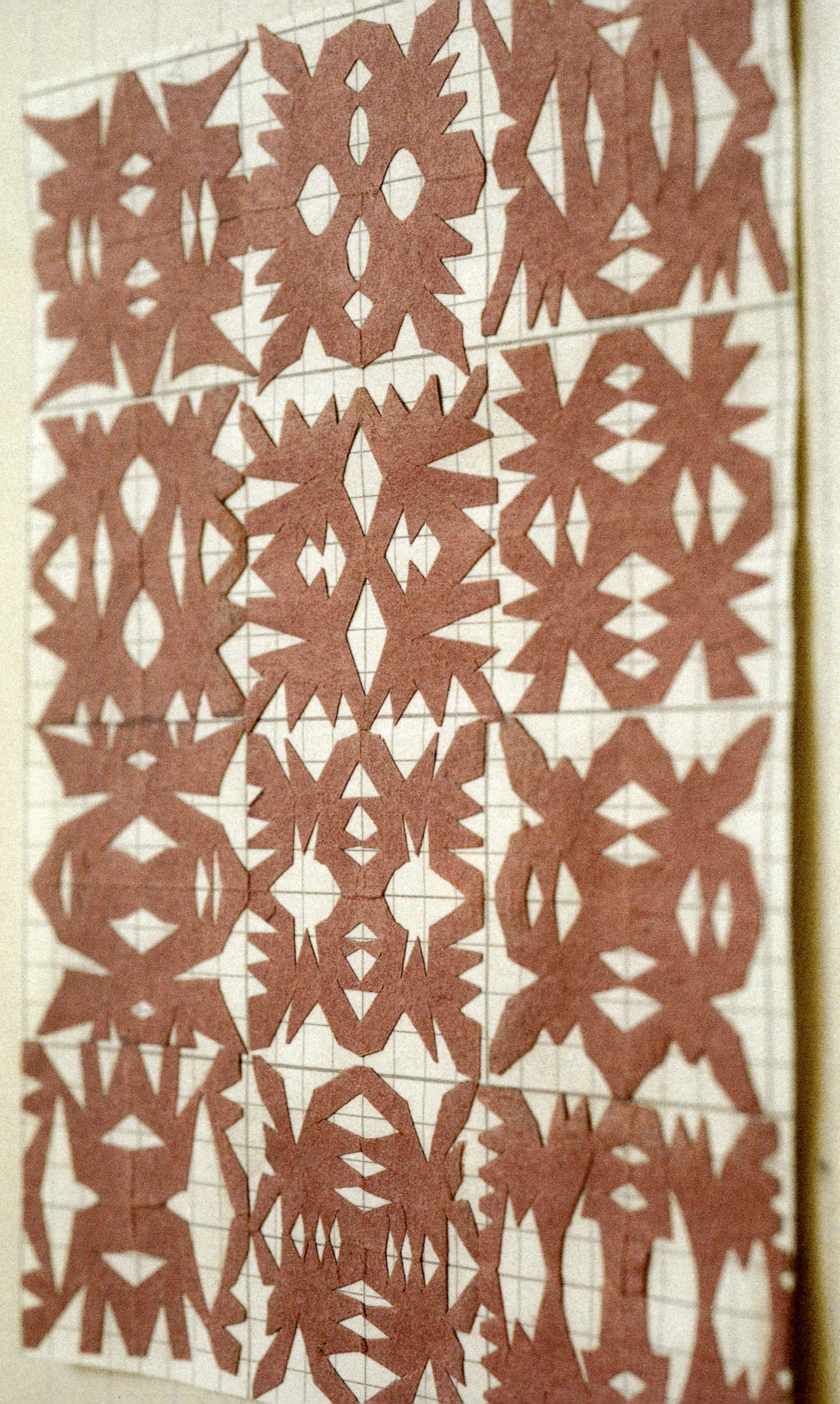

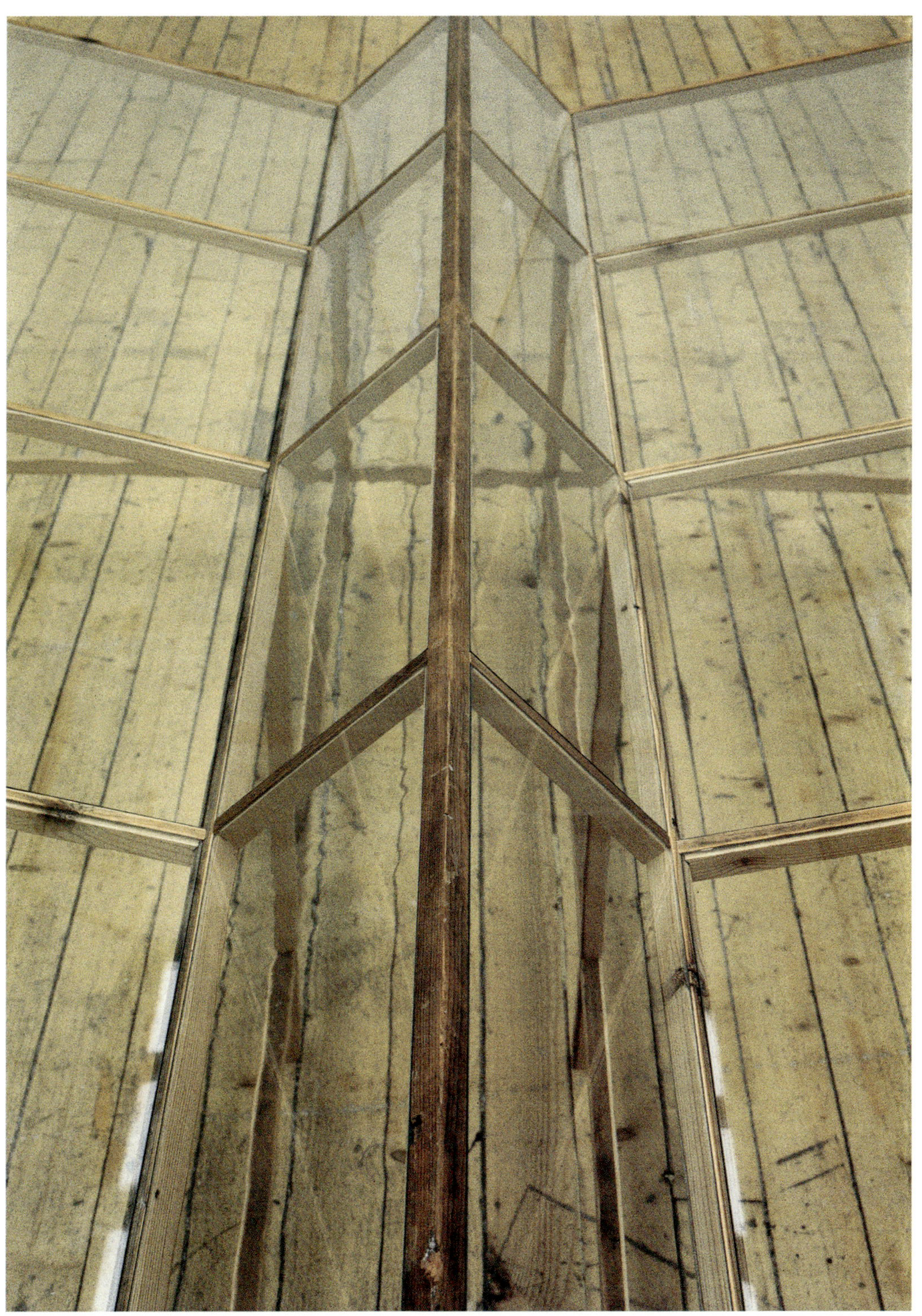

AH   It's interesting that you think of temperature because, for
          me, this is relevant to the process of making; the way the
          materials behave – for example, the way plaster heats up
          before it sets. But I think there's also a certain feeling – I can't
          really use the word 'energy'. But I'd like to think there's a
          circulation taking place that, at times, is slowed down or
          speeded up. There's a sense of flux, of temperature, rising
          and falling. I'm not sure I would separate that idea from its
          physical nature – to use it solely as a metaphor for mood.
          It has more to do with that organic nature of space that
          we've been talking about. On the level of vegetation,
          plants – what do you need for things to grow? Light,
          water, temperature. For me, that's a principle that's
          present throughout the work.

FB   In that sense, are *Geraniums* triggers or some kind of clue
          to your intentions?

AH   Maybe they are. They were a very direct way of relating to
          the gallery space. A large part of what I do is growing
          things. I like the greenness and the light, the translucency
          of the leaves, the ability of the plant to expel scent – like an
          offer, it breathes out at it's own pace. There's something
          startling, or at least unexpected, in that. For me that green
          is an essential condition.

FB   The plants seem to generate a sense of proximity and touch
          that influences how we look and respond physically to the
          other pieces in the exhibition.

AH   There's also a strong element of touch in the work. It
          comes through the process of making and the vulnerabilities
          that come with that process. Some pieces can't shake off
          their initial clumsiness – sometimes they're made quickly,
          sometimes, they take a long time. There's a level – which

isn't perfection – that has more to do with the concentration
of touch, and that can mean a very rough edge or a very
smooth edge. The materials have gone through a process –
a transformation, or sometimes just the passing of time.
In the casting process, it moves from dry to wet to a solid
substance. Other materials are used, found or given to me
– and they carry their own histories with them, their own
particularities. So in a way, as objects, they anchor time and
gather meaning because they are used. The piece, *Bench*
(pp. 45, 53), describes the relationship between one thing
and another and the space between the two. The space is
shared and bridged. To me it represents a very happy
moment and the desire for a kind of timelessness.

FB   The work sometimes has a metaphorical resonance, yet other
times it's more concrete – like *Glasshouse* (pp. 23, 29, 41, 43, 49).

AH   Some of the pieces are, at first, very tangible – although they
may carry different identities. *Glasshouse* might be a museum
cabinet, a greenhouse, a coldframe, an architectural model for
a building, etc. These identities seem to cancel each other out.
What's left is a container that reflects its surroundings – a
space that condenses energy but also allows it to pass through.
Like a balloon, it floats just above the ground. The work
becomes an imaginary space, a state of mind or condition.

The piece *Shelter* (pages 18, 19, 21, 35) – two models of
rudimentary buildings – function in a similar way. As models,
they're already encompassing the desire to make something
possible that is abstract or even ideal. In order for the model
then to become something real – something you live and work
with – the ideal must become concrete and you have to use your
imagination to bring this about. In the best moments, I think
the work waivers between an abstract and a concrete space.

FB   The idea of the model as a concrete reality seems also to
relate to the photograph that you used for the invitation
to the exhibition, *Brighton Pier* (p. 75).

AH   I like that image very much. It was given to me and I pass
it on as such. It describes a moment where something is
illuminated. You come across something and, in an instant
of unexpected recognition, it alters your perception – and
your frame of mind. The model of the West Pier – which
looks like a spaceship that's just landed – becomes a means
of transportation.

FB   You have talked at other times of 'moment' as a defining
element in your work.

AH   When I use the word, 'moment' here, I think particularly
of Clarice Lispector's, *The Hour of the Star*, where she
describes an instant as the *"particle of time in which
the tyre of a car going at full speed touches the ground,
touches it no longer, then touches it again"*.[†]

"– As for the future." are the last words of the main
character, at the end of the story, before she dies. They
describe a very particular moment which is absolute –
'now' – but it also makes a spark between the future
and the past, the ending and the beginning.

† From *The Hour of the Star* by Clarice Lispector, trans. Giovanni Pontiero, Carcanet Press, 1986.

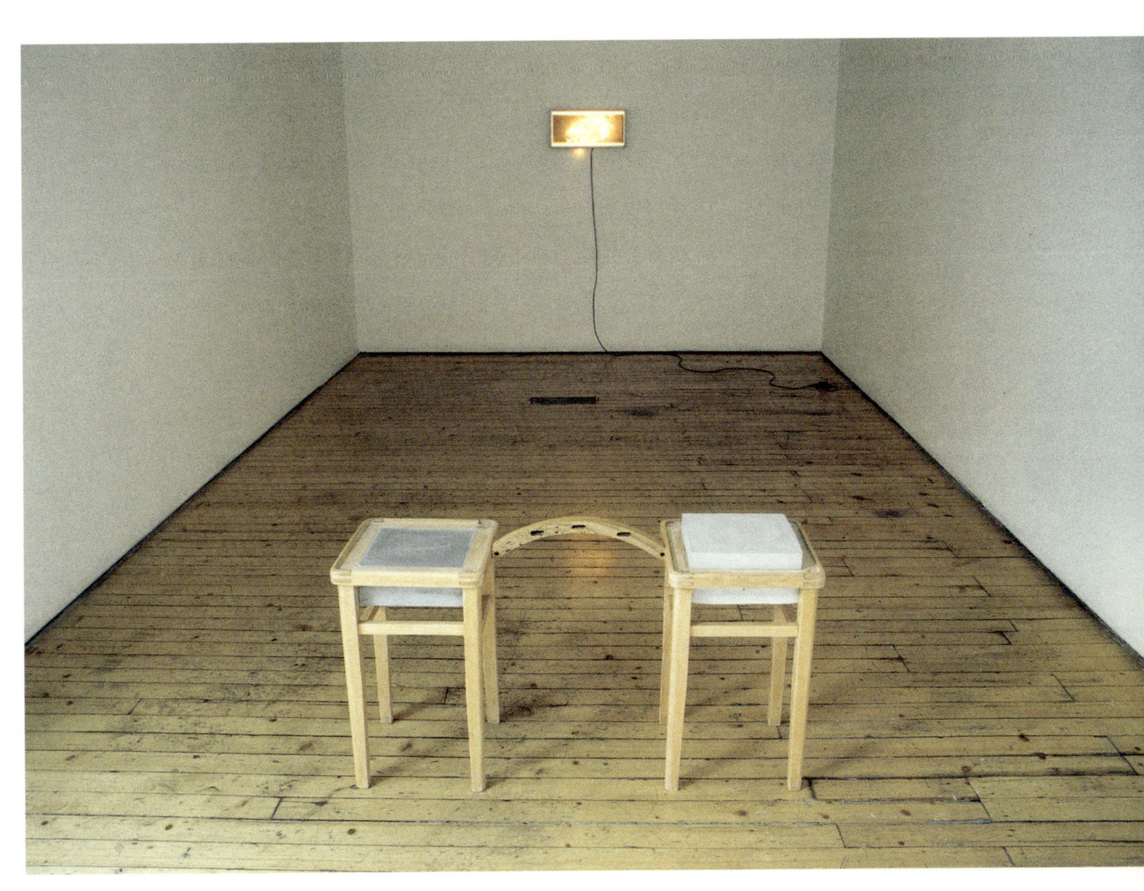

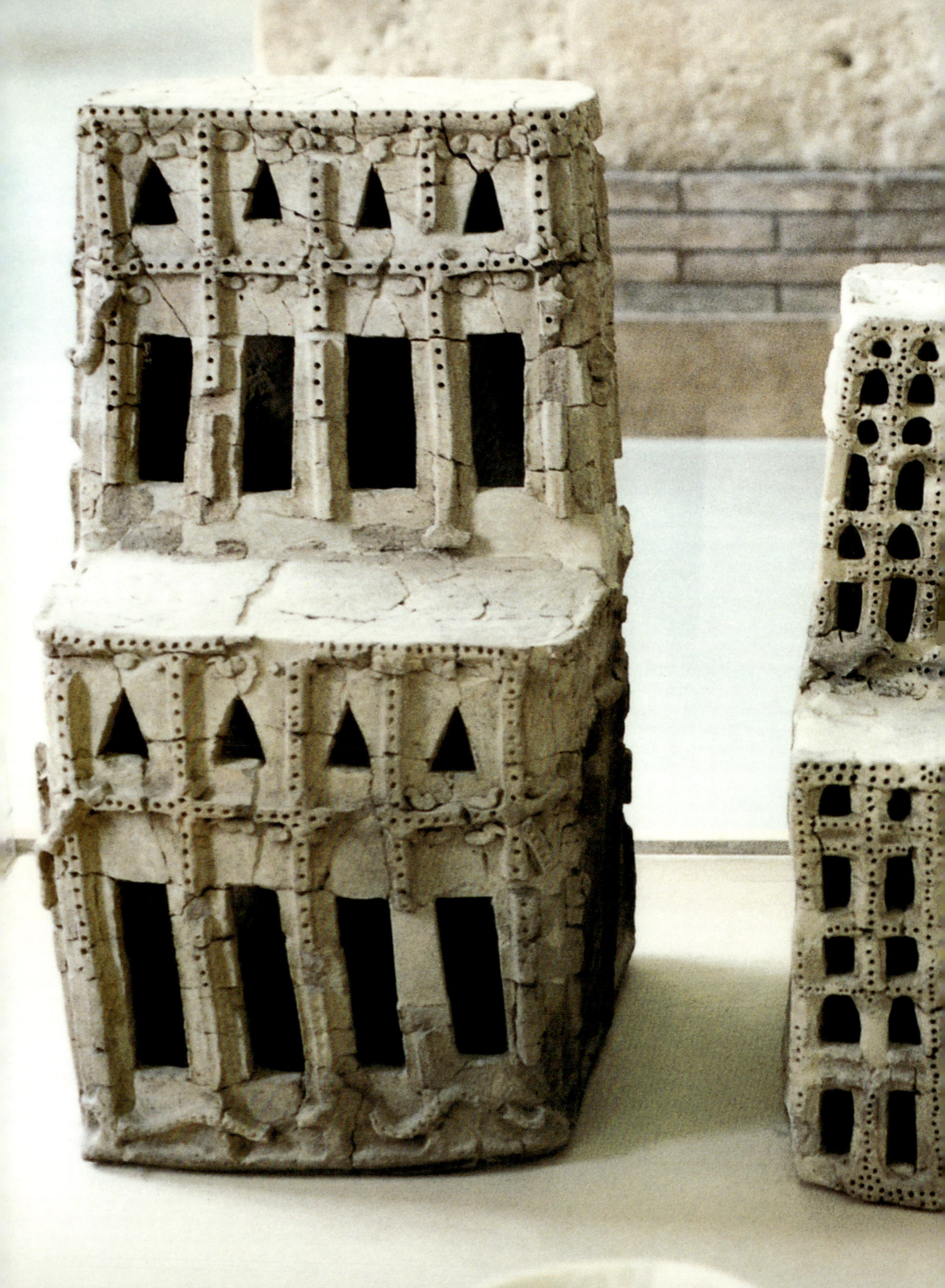

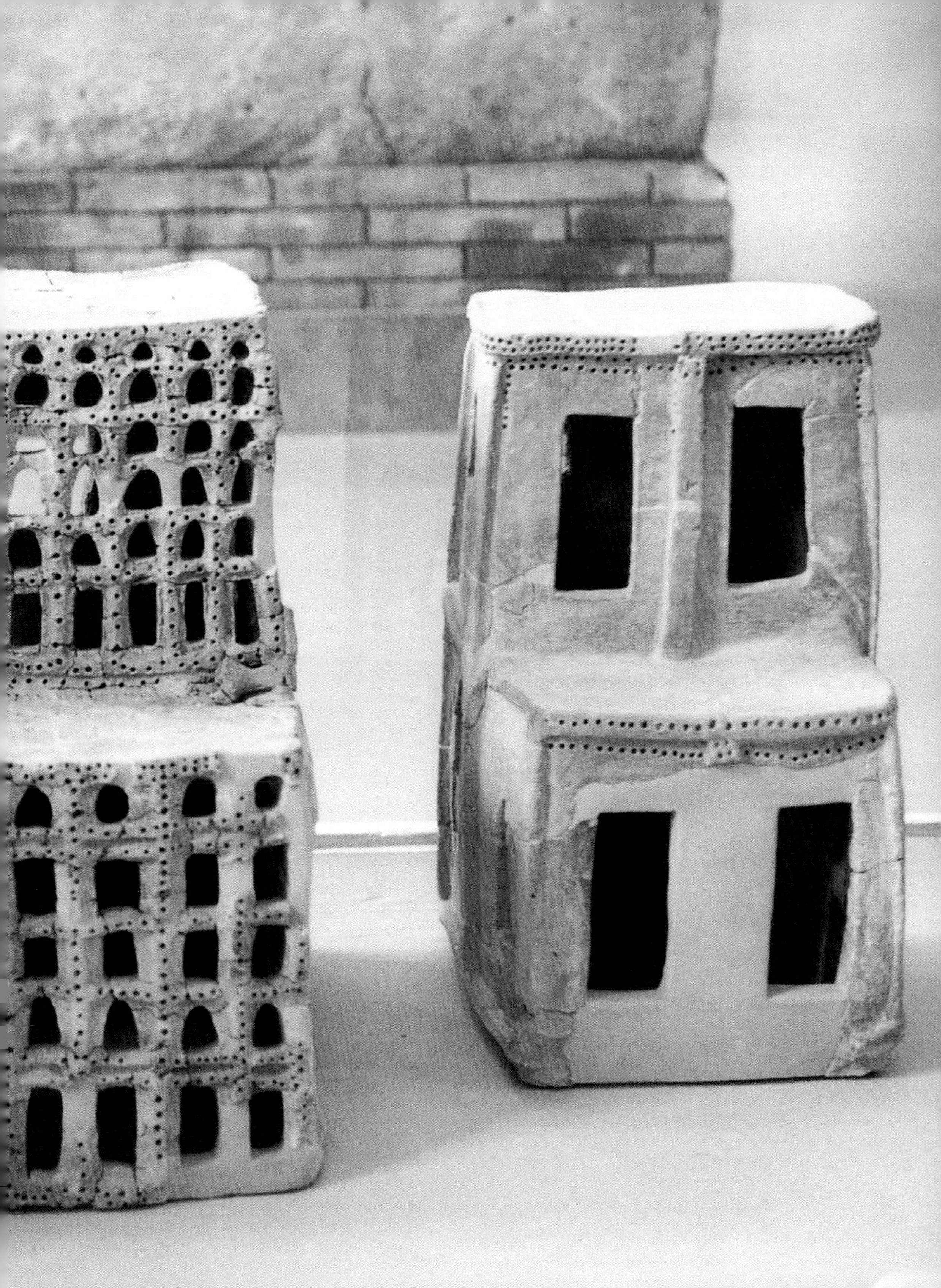

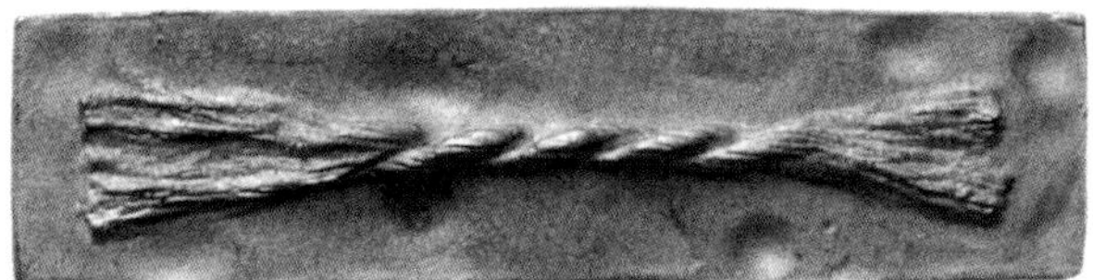
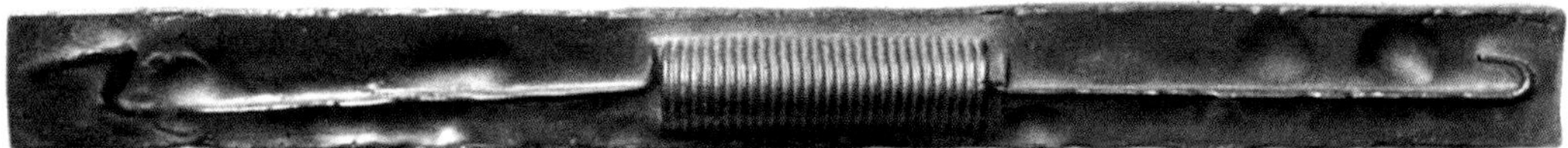

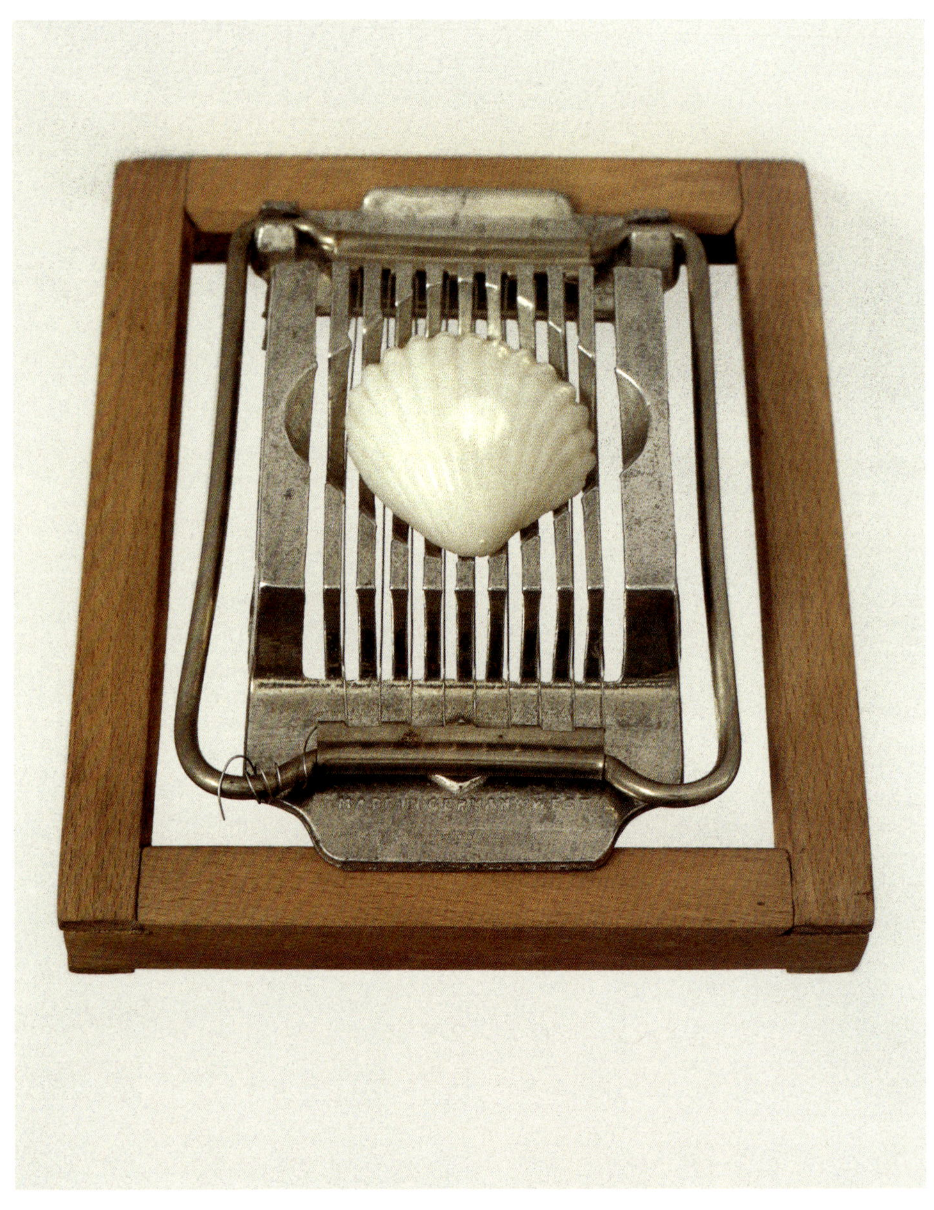

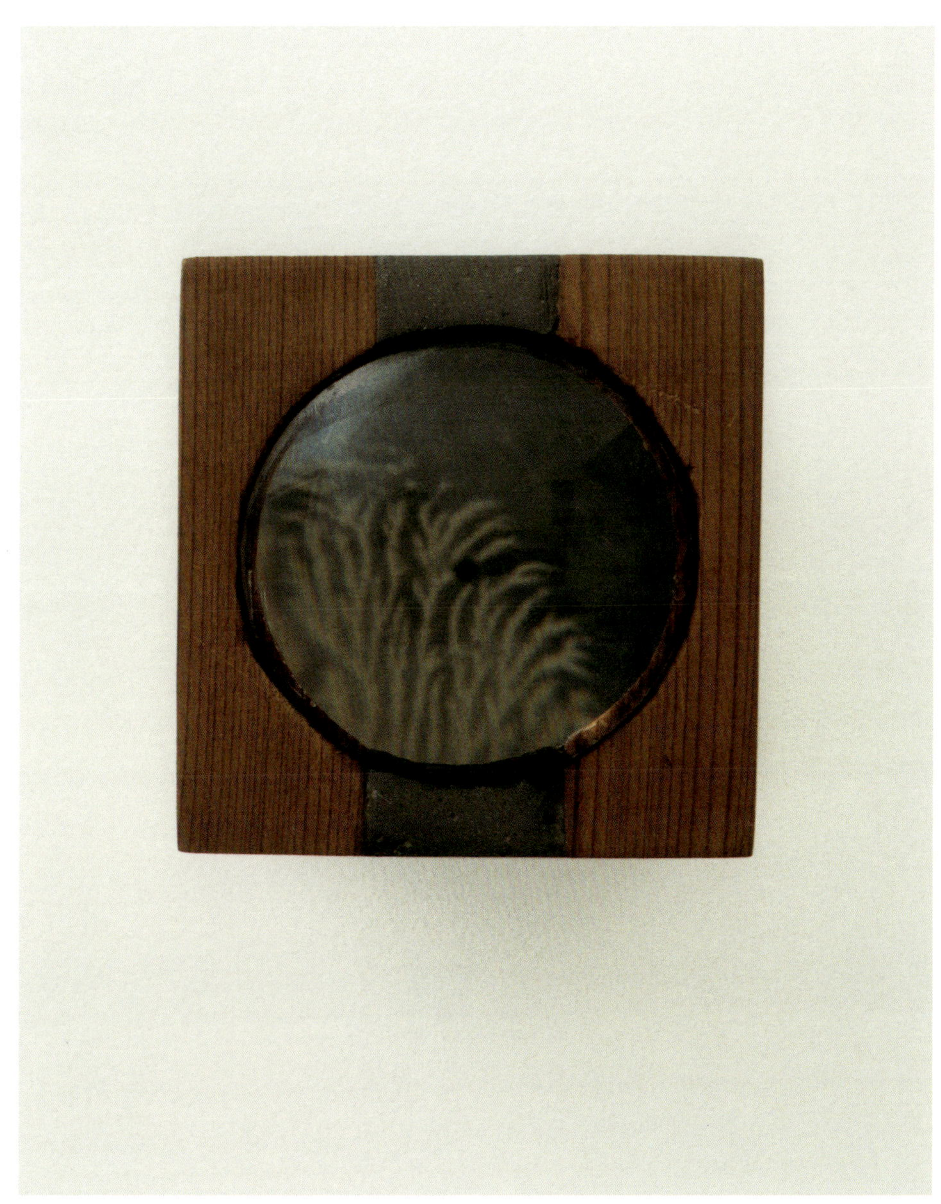

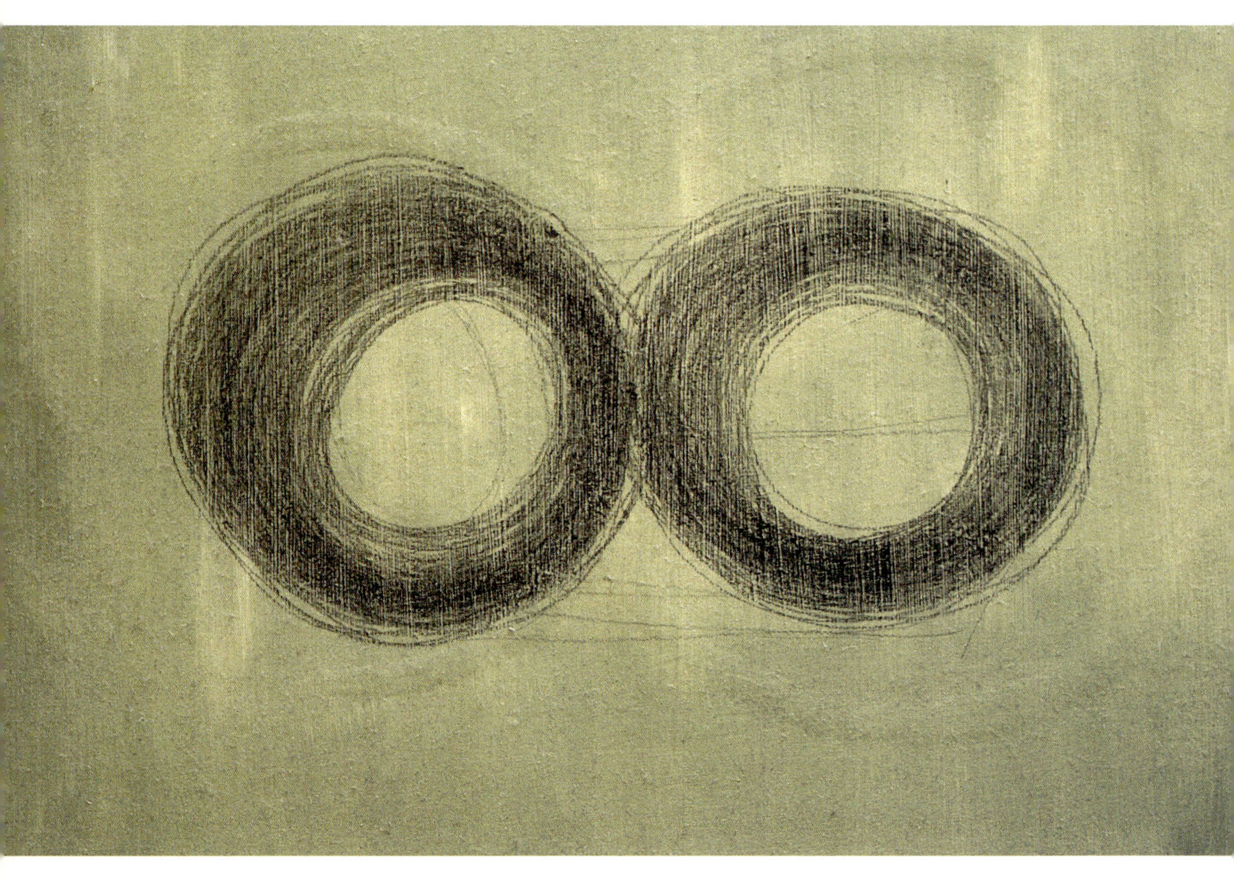

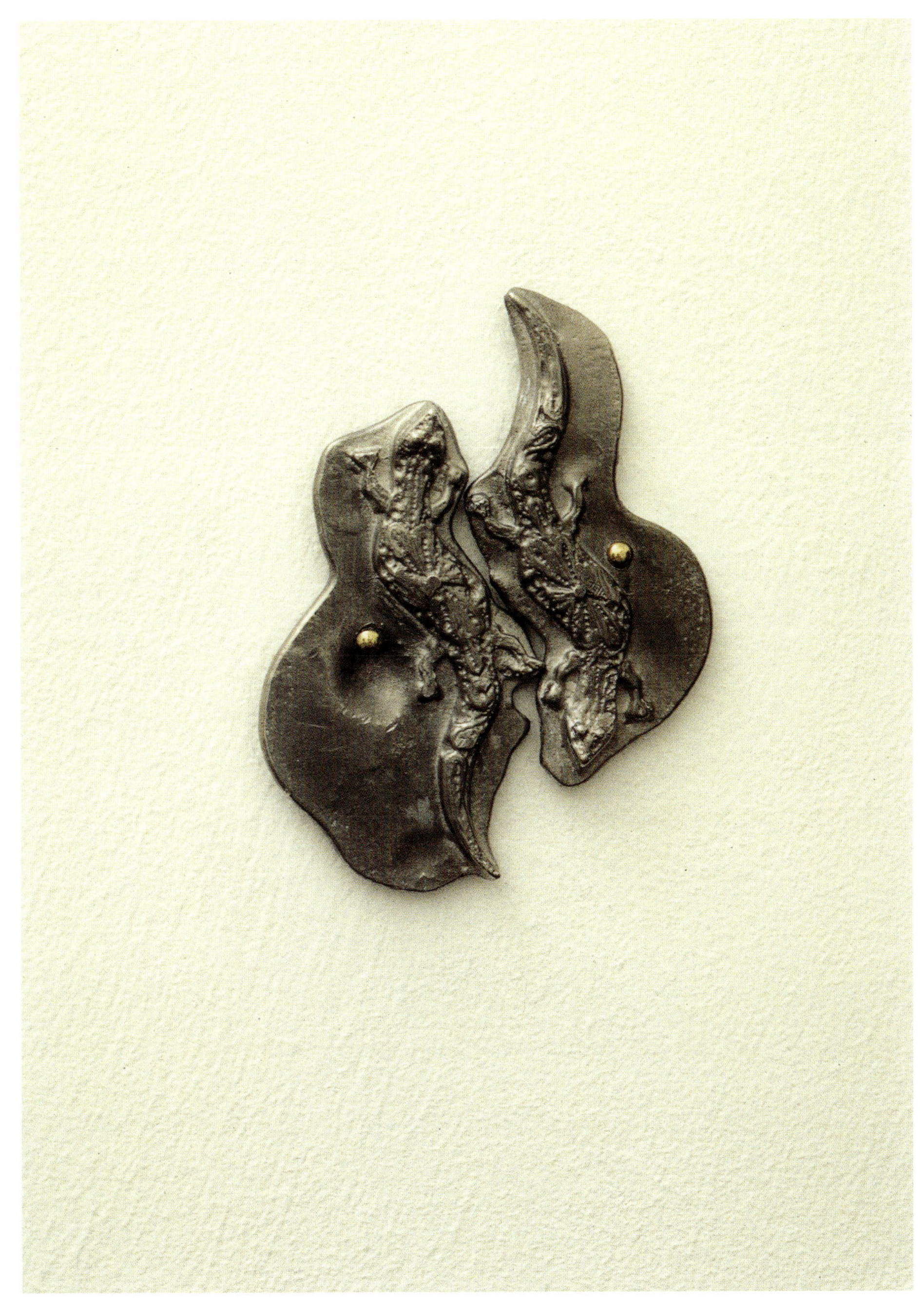

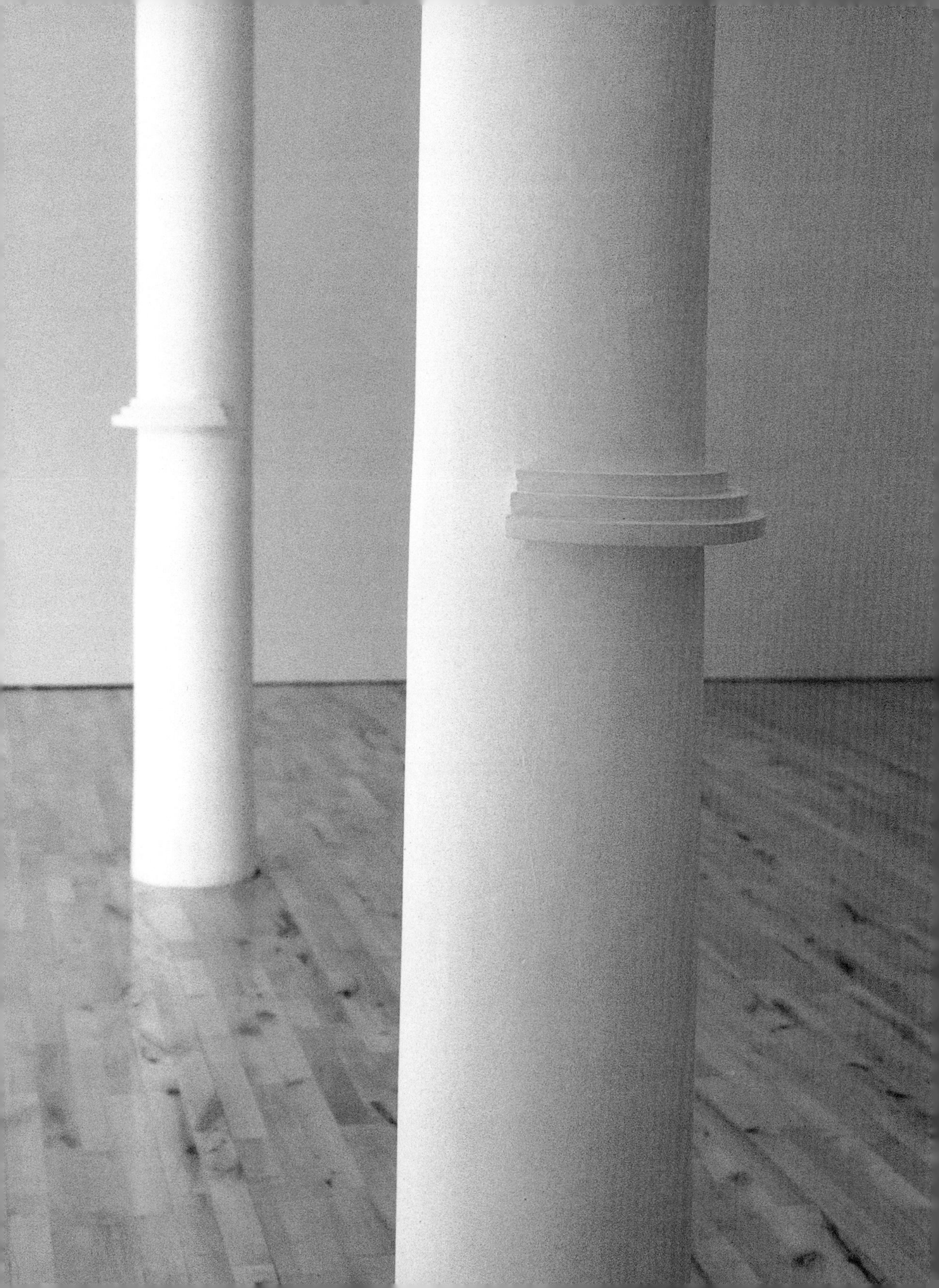

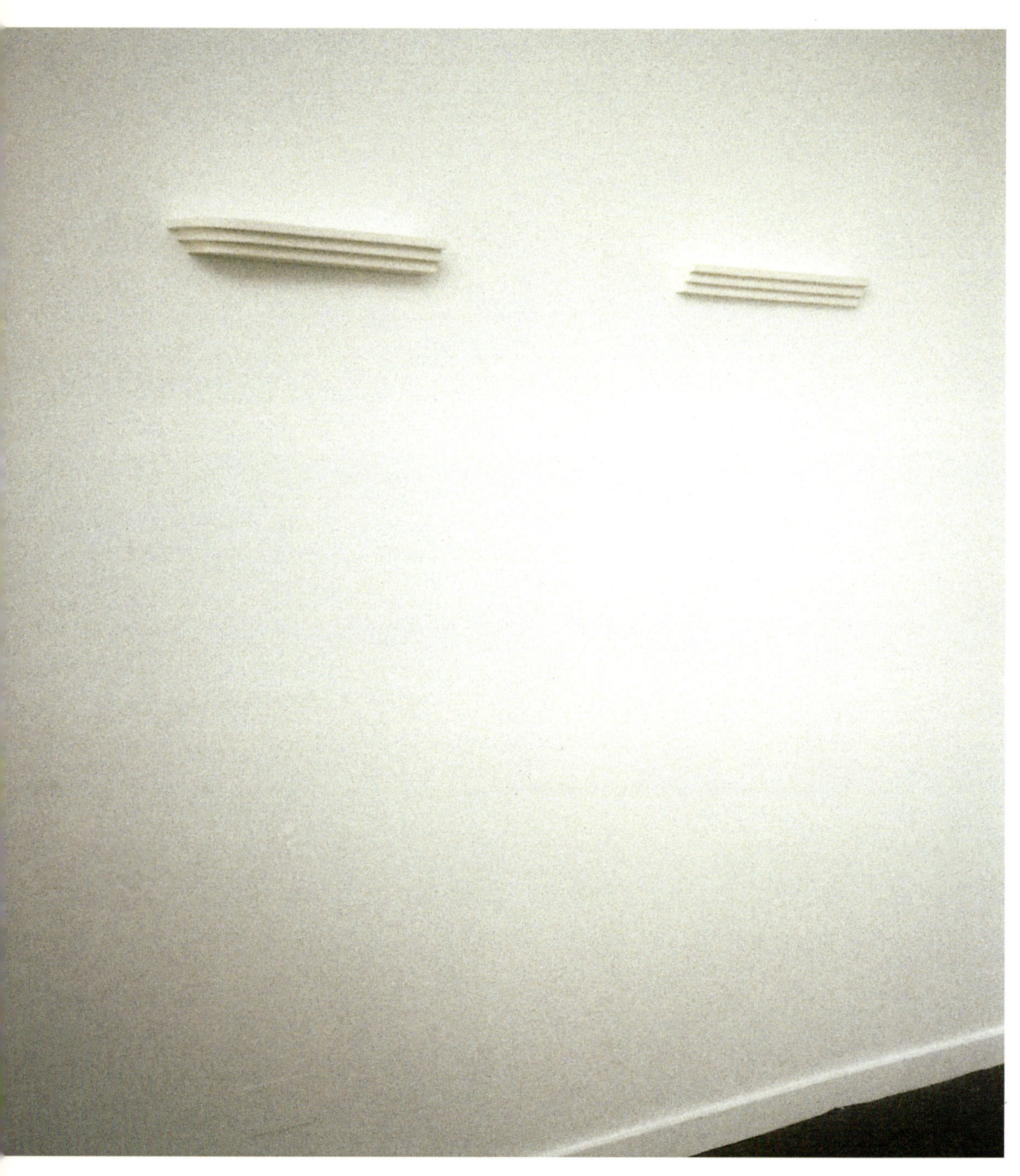

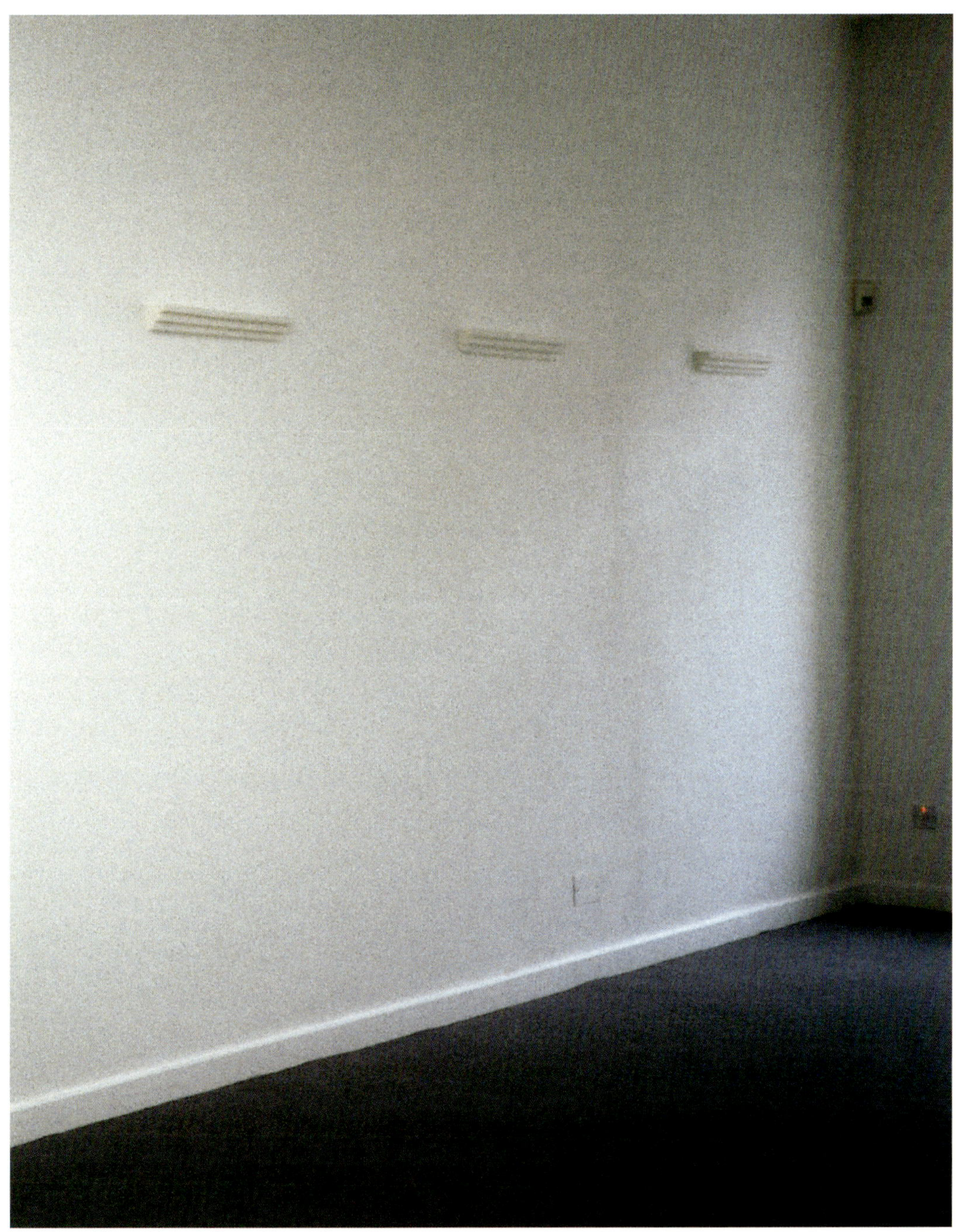

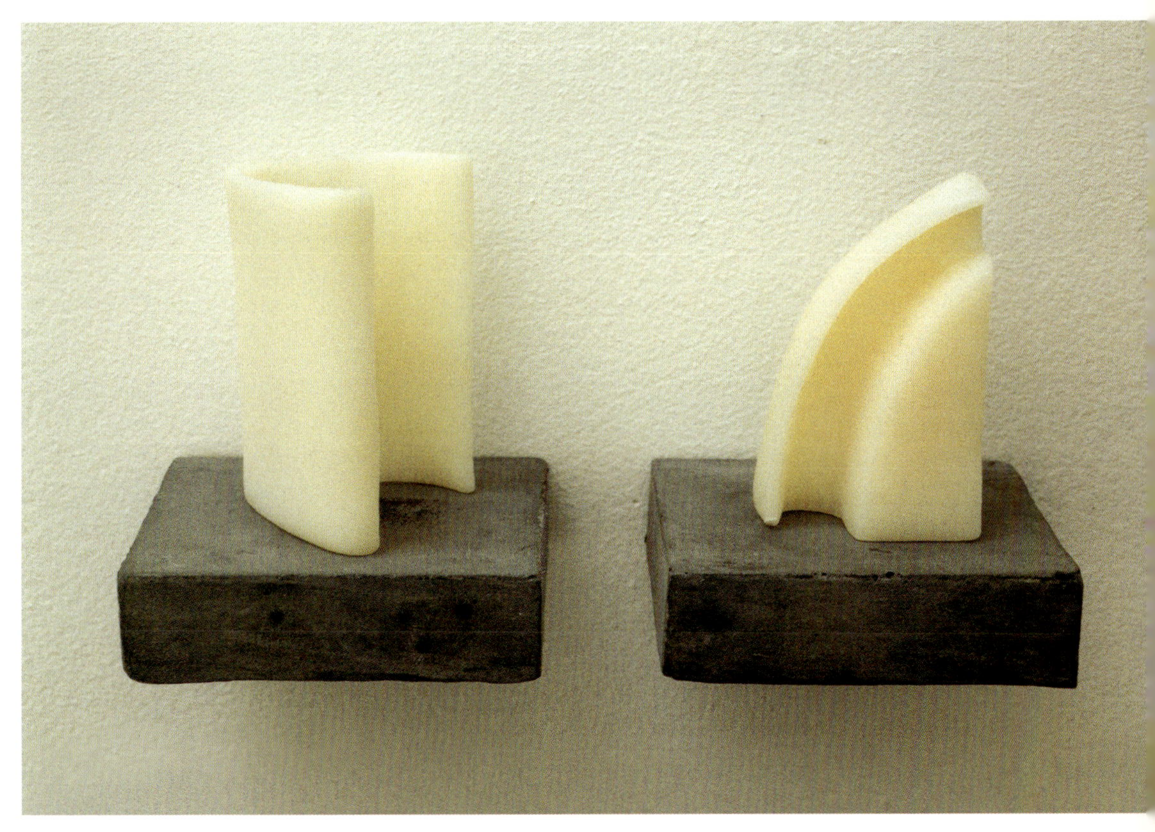

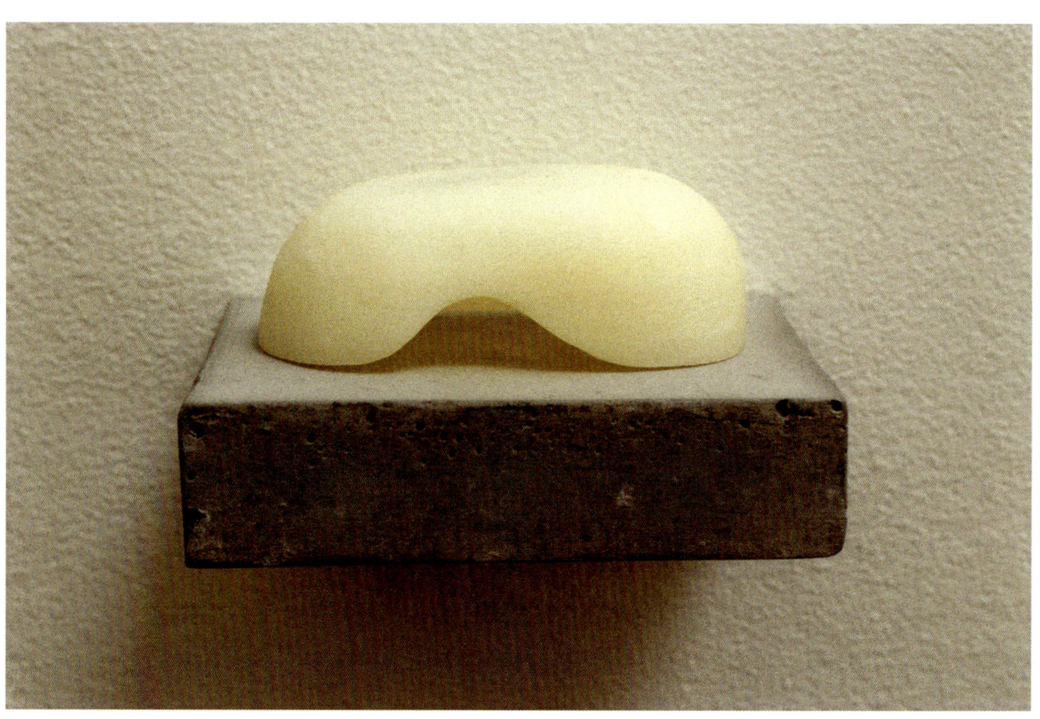

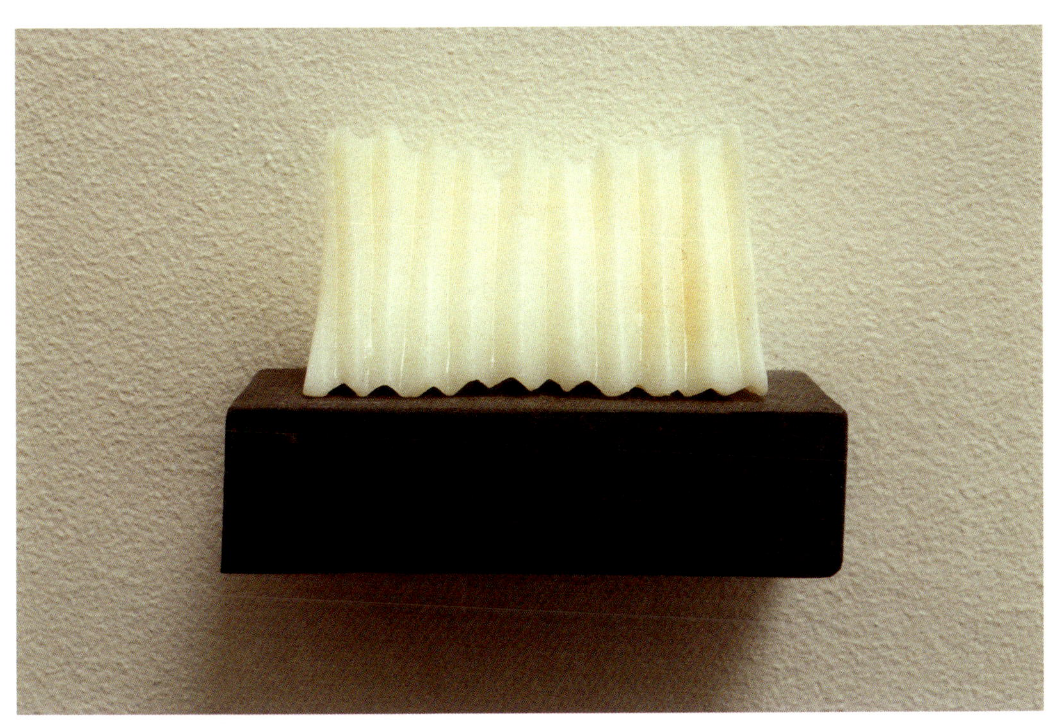

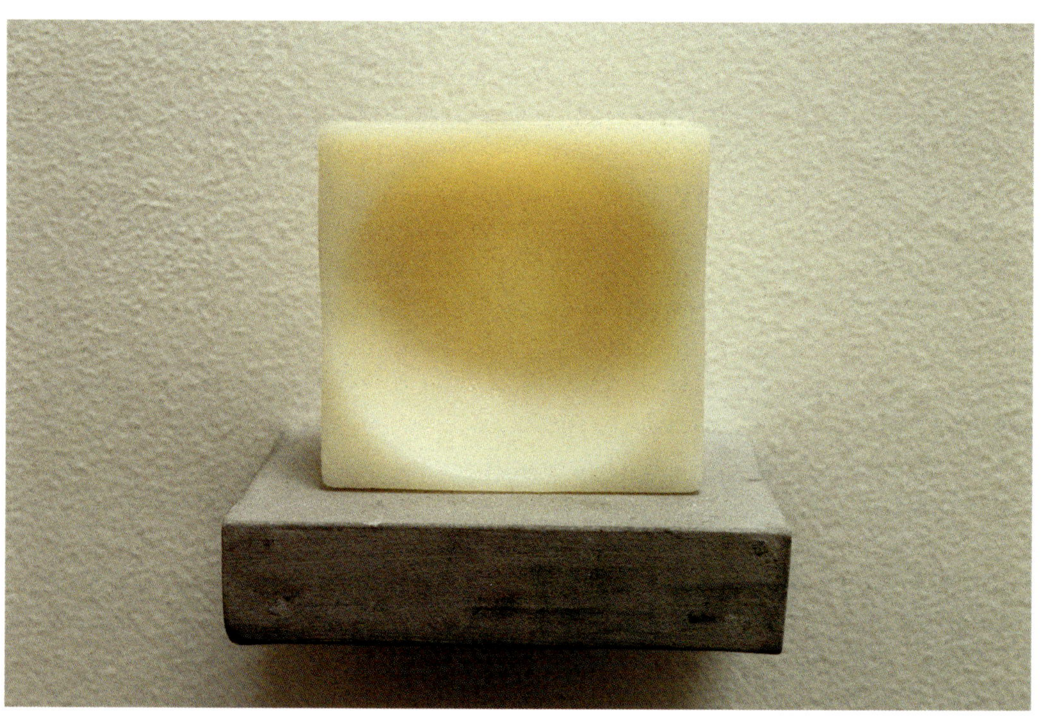

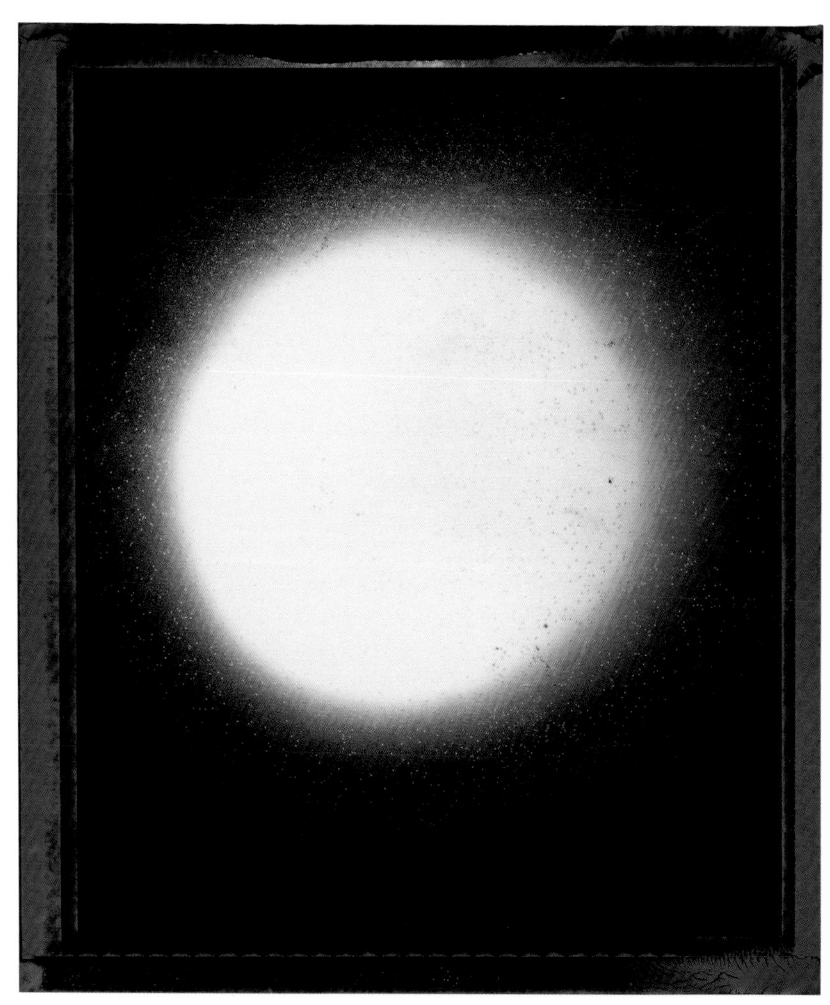

List of illustrations

Cover   *Geranium;* silver gelatine print; Linlithgow, 2000

Page 3   *Geraniums (detail);* The Fruitmarket Gallery, Edinburgh, 2000

Page 4   *Untitled*; Polaroid; Linlithgow, 2000

Page 5   *Silverpoint Drawing*; Oriel Mostyn Gallery, Llandudno, 1994

Page 6   *Concrete Cast I*; silver gelatine print; 2000

Page 7   *Concrete Cast II*; silver gelatine print; 2000

Page 8-9   *Shadow*; silver gelatine print; 2000

Page 10   *Wall*; silver gelatine print; 2000

Page 11   *Concrete Cast*; installation; The Fruitmarket Gallery, Edinburgh, 2000

Page 12   *Silverpoint Drawing*; Oriel Mostyn Gallery, Llandudno, 1994

Page 13   *Staircase*; silver gelatine print; Street Level Gallery, Glasgow, 1996

Page 14   *Corridor*; silver gelatine print; 1997

Page 15   *Cerberus*; silver gelatine print; 2000

Page 17   *Corner*; silver gelatine print; 2000

Page 18   *Shelter*; cast plaster, stone-cutter's table; The Fruitmarket Gallery, Edinburgh, 2000

Pages 19 & 21 *Shelter (detail)*

Page 22   *Geraniums*; oak working table, flower pots, lemon geraniums; The Fruitmarket Gallery, Edinburgh, 2000

Page 23   *Glasshouse (detail)*; The Fruitmarket Gallery, Edinburgh, 2000

Page 24-25 *Greenhouse*; colour photograph; West Lothian, 2000

Page 26   *Ink Drawing;* 1999

Page 29   *Glasshouse*; Douglas Fir, greenhouse glass; The Fruitmarket Gallery, Edinburgh, 2000

Page 32   *Concrete Cast*; installation; The Fruitmarket Gallery, Edinburgh, 2000

Page 33   *Geraniums*; installation; The Fruitmarket Gallery, Edinburgh, 2000

Page 35   *Shelter*; The Fruitmarket Gallery, Edinburgh, 2000

Page 38   *Cerberus*; silver gelatine print; The Fruitmarket Gallery, Edinburgh, 2000

Page 41   *Glasshouse (detail)*; The Fruitmarket Gallery, Edinburgh, 2000

Page 42   *Papercut (detail)*; Fordham Gallery, London, 1999

Page 43   *Glasshouse (detail)*, The Fruitmarket Gallery, Edinburgh, 2000

Page 44   *Lightbox*; metal box, strip light, duratran; The Fruitmarket Gallery,
                 Edinburgh, 2000

Page 45   *Bench*; beechwood stools, oak backrest, cast plaster;
                 The Fruitmarket Gallery, Edinburgh, 2000

Page 47   *Papercut Drawing I*; 1999

Page 48   *Papercut Drawing II*; 1999

Page 49   *Glasshouse (detail)*; The Fruitmarket Gallery, Edinburgh, 2000

Page 53   *Bench and Lightbox*; The Fruitmarket Gallery, Edinburgh, 2000

Page 54-55   *Prayer stools*; colour photograph; Pergamon Museum, Berlin, 1999

Page 56   *String – Spring*; cast zinc; Street Level Gallery, Glasgow, 1996

Page 57   *Possil South East*; silver gelatine print; Oriel Mostyn Gallery,
                 Llandudno, 1994

Page 58   *Cataract* (from the series *Instruments of Precision*); wood, lenses;
                 Galerie Giselle Linder, Basle, 1995

Page 59   *Egg Cutter* (from the series *Instruments of Precision*); plastic shell,
                 egg-cutter, contact frame; Street Level Gallery, Glasgow, 1996

Page 60   *Circles*; oil paint and pencil on canvas; 2000

Page 61   *Lizards*; cast zinc; Street Level Gallery, Glasgow, 1996

Page 63   *Columns*; cast plaster; Street Level Gallery, Glasgow, 1996

Pages 64-65   *Untitled I*; cast plaster; Angel Row Gallery, Nottingham, 1998

Page 67   *Untitled II*; cast plaster; Angel Row Gallery, Nottingham, 1998

Pages 68-70   *Recurring Shapes*; carved soap, plaster shelf; Angel Row Gallery,
                 Nottingham, 1998

Page 71   *Moon*; silver gelatine print; Oriel Mostyn Gallery, Llandudno, 1994

Page 75   *Brighton Pier (model)*; colour photograph; Brighton, 2000

All photographs made by Annette Heyer, except *Brighton Pier* (anonymous).

Annette Heyer

Born in Hamburg, 1960. Based in Scotland.

Solo Exhibitions

2000   – *As for the future.*, The Fruitmarket Gallery, Edinburgh

1998   *New Work*, Angel Row Gallery, Nottingham

1996   *New Work*, Street Level Gallery, Glasgow

Group Exhibitions

1999   *Unreal City*, Fordham Gallery, London
Readymade Project, Wunderkammer, London
Flesh and Stone, Fordham Gallery, London

1998   *Wysiwyg*, Baconfieldstudio, Brighton

1997   *Wysiwyg*, Miedzynarodowe Centrum, Poznan

1996   *Durchröntgen*, Art & Rat Gallerie, Remscheid
Viewfinder, Grange Courtyard, Linlithgow

1995   Gallery Exhibition, Galerie Gisele Linder, Basle
Decade, Street Level Gallery, Glasgow

1994   *Riviera*, Oriel Mostyn Gallery, Llandudno

1993   *Aqua Vitae*, Stills Gallery, Edinburgh

1992   *With Attitude*, Contretype, Brussels
Transmission at City Racing, City Racing Gallery, London
Mai de la Photo, Reims
Outta Here, Transmission Gallery, Glasgow
Other Dimensions, Stills Gallery, Edinburgh

Acknowledgments

I would like to thank Graeme Murray and The Fruitmarket Gallery, John Calcutt and Glasgow School of Art, Fine Art Photography Department.

I also want to thank my friends, both here and there, for their continuous help and support – Jim Hamlyn, Lise Bratton, David Bellingham, John Nichol, David Harrison, Heather McDonough, Franziska Bark, Swantje Werner, Johannes Buck and, especially my mother, Heike Heyer.

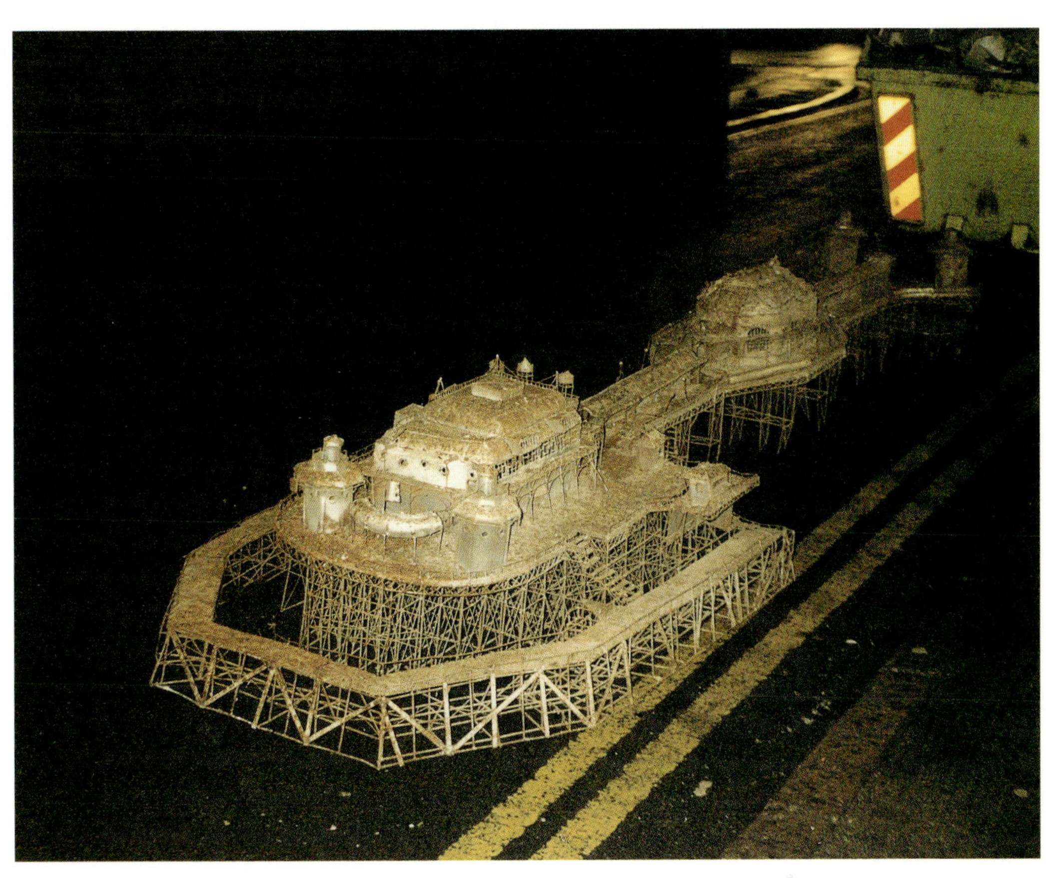

This book was published to accompany Annette Heyer's exhibition
– *As For the Future.* at The Fruitmarket Gallery, Edinburgh,
7 October to 18 November 2000. The exhibition formed the third
part of *Visions for the Future*, a project initiated by The Fruitmarket Gallery
to commission and exhibit new bodies of work by Scotland-based artists.

Exhibition funded by The Esmée Fairbairn Charitable Trust and
The Robertson Trust.

Publication funded by The Henry Moore Foundation and
The Glasgow School of Art.

John Calcutt is a writer and Lecturer at Glasgow School of Art.

Designed by Annette Heyer and Lise Bratton and set by
Lise Bratton, Ultramarine *Vermilion*, Edinburgh.

Published by The Fruitmarket Gallery, 45 Market Street, Edinburgh EH1 1DF.
Tel: 0131 225 2383 Fax: 0131 220 3130. Website: www.fruitmarket.co.uk

The Fruitmarket Gallery is subsidised by the Scottish Arts Council.
Scottish Charity No. SC 005576.

Printed in an edition of 1,000 copies by specialblue, London.
Printed in the UK. ISBN 0 947912 92 4

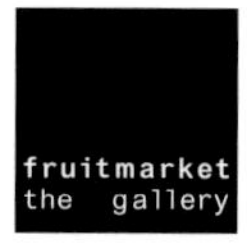

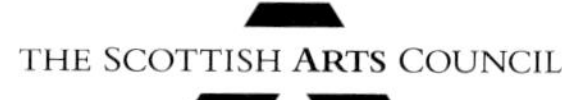